Working the Land: Building a Life

By Fran Cirbo

Enjoy!
Fran Cirbo

Working the Land:
Building a Life

Fran Cirbo
francirbo@aol.com

FELLTTA Books
ISBN 978-0-615-31801-1
www.pochettebooks.com/francirbo.htm
printed in the United States ©2009

Dedication

I dedicate this book to my children

Betty, Teri, (Veronica)
Tom Jr. Leo, Larry and
Anthony (deceased)

Acknowledgements

I would like to thank all the people who have helped me with this book. I owe a special thanks to the people in Heather Gardens Writers Club for their constant encouragement to stay with it until the end. A special thanks to the past instructor of Writer's Club, Doreen Pollock-Kreh, and our instructor Chuck Pierce. Special thanks to Pat Quinlan and Forest McClure of Writer's Club for editing, layouts and working with the photos.

Thanks to my children who were especially helpful and supportive. They helped me to become computer savvy, coached and coaxed me. I appreciate the help and support from my many relatives and friends.

Prologue

Andrew and Lucy Kochis were pioneers on the Colorado Plains. They were my parents, and this is their story. The first chapter begins with their life in Europe. The second chapter is about the first few years in America, before they moved to Colorado. The third chapter is about their life on the homestead. The remainder of the book pertains to the living conditions and how these European immigrants survived on the eastern plains of Colorado in the early 1900's. Most of this book was told to me by my mother in March of 1975. She was ninety years old.

Mother believed in living for today and tomorrow so getting her to talk about the "old days" was difficult. She was reluctant to discuss her past. I was fortunate when my daughter Teri was to write an essay for class on someone "old and famous" from Elbert County. This is a very sparsely populated area so there were few famous people from which to choose. There was no one we thought of as famous, so my daughter chose to write about her grandmother. As we asked questions my mother shared what her life was like in Europe. She told us of those early years with her family when she arrived in America. If it had not been for that school project I wouldn't have a story to tell.

I was the youngest child born to parents who emigrated from what is now Slovakia and homesteaded on the Colorado plains. They brought with them the customs of their country. Mom described life in the village of Rudnik, in what was Austria-Hungary and some of the things that happened here in America.

The last part of this book contains my recollections and those of my siblings and other relatives. I have described the details of farming in those days as well as how life has changed throughout the years.

I hope you enjoy this story as much as I did when my mother told it to us.

Table of Contents

My Family Tree

Name	Birthday	Married	Died
Andy Kochis	Nov. 19, 1874	July 13, 1902	March 20, 1962
Lucy Radacy	Dec. 11, 1884		March 1, 1981
John Kochis	April 25,1903	Nov. 2, 1934	Jan. 22, 1990
Ruth Wilson	Sept. 20,1916		Feb. 11, 1998
Kate Kochis	May 2, 1905	July 27, 1936	March 21, 2003
Ted Flinn	Oct. 1, 1894		Sept. 30, 1990
Andy Kochis	May 10, 1909		6 month old
Paul Kochis	June 29, 1907		April 18, 1974
Andy Kochis	Jan. 4, 1909	Jan. 7, 1941	July 27, 1986
Mildred Cirbo	Aug. 8, 1922		July 30, 1998
Ann Kochis	Feb. 22, 1911	June 17, 1941	May 20, 1980
Art Roberts	Sept .12, 1910		Aug. 17, 1992
Joe Kochis	Dec. 18, 1912		July 19, 1925
Frank Kochis	Aug. 19, 1914	Aug. 6, 1946	Oct. 29, 1967
Mary M			
Helen Kochis	June 18, 1916	Aug. 24, 1941	
George Franek	June 7, 1913		Jan. 28, 1988
George Kochis	Oct. 26, 1917		Nov. 25, 1920
Mike Kochis	Jan. 8, 1920		March 24, 1922
Steve Kochis	Aug. 17, 1921	July 1, 1943	
Leona Gimera	Sept. 23, 1917		Aug. 17, 1984
Mary Kochis	Dec. 16, 1923	Feb. 18, 1942	
Paul Manyik	June 25, 1912		Sept. 20, 1966
Frances Kochis	Nov. 2, 1927	Dec. 1, 1945	
Thomas Cirbo	Jan. 15, 1924		

Czechoslovakia

My Mother (Lucy Radacy) and Father (Andrew Kochis) were born in Rudnik, Austria-Hungary. After World War I it was renamed Czechoslovakia.

Many of the small towns in Europe had a church located in the center or on the town square. Religion was very important and was the focus of social life. On Sunday afternoons the children attended religious services. In Rudnik the only church was a Catholic church. There was only one general store where everything that the villagers couldn't grow was purchased. There was only one school and the children were required to be seven years old by September 1st. Their highest education was the sixth grade.

When a son married and remained in Europe he stayed in the same town because that is where he was employed. He built a house at the back of his parent's lot and the animals were kept between the houses. The next son to get married built a house across the street facing his brother's house. The third son built at the back of that brother's house.

The houses and barns were made of adobe blocks and were attached to each other. To make blocks, fine straw was mixed with adobe mud. The oxen trampled the straw and adobe by being led in a circle until it was blended together. It was poured into boxes and set to dry. After the blocks were dry and ready for use they were set in place as cement blocks or bricks are today. More wet adobe was used as mortar to hold them in place.

The rooms in the homes were twenty feet square. A bedroom was on one side of the kitchen and a storage room on the other. This storage room was used as a pantry and tool shed. During summer the tools were kept outside and most of the food was consumed during the winter months. They used the storage room for a bedroom the rest of the summer. The mattresses were made of straw and there were no bedsprings. (Even in America on the homestead and the home-place they had straw mattresses for many years.) The floors of the house were dirt. To seal the cracks in the floor a thick paste was made by mixing manure and water together, spreading it on the floor. This made the floors smooth.

Each building had an awning ten feet wide to keep the rain and snow from washing the adobe walls away. A twenty-foot awning was on the front of the house. The children's play area was under the awnings so the family could keep an eye on the toddlers.

There were no fences and the wells were not covered. There were no cellars because the water table was very high. The Radacy's well was so shallow they knelt down and dipped in the bucket. To get water from the neighboring wells a rope was tied to a bucket and lowered into the well. A stick was used to tip the bucket to fill it with water.

The only animals confined were the chickens. There were no corrals. The barn was attached to the back of the house and divided into several sections. One section was used to keep the calf from the cow so the family could take enough milk for their use. There were different sections for the oxen and pigs. There was a smokehouse used for smoking the hams, shoulders, bacon and sausage. The outhouse was close to the manure pile.

All tools such as the rake, hoe, shovel and pitch fork were made of wood. One piece of machinery was a walking plow pulled by a team of oxen. Weeds were not a problem. Metal tools were introduced before Mom and Dad moved to America.

There was only one field for the entire village. Each family was responsible for their own crops in their designated space. The crops planted were wheat, oats, barley, millet and rye. These were the only seeds that were available and the ones the farmers knew about at that time. A few rows of corn were planted only for their consumption because space was limited. To plant grain in the field they took a handful of seeds and tossed it over the prepared ground (called broadcasting). It was important to know how thick or thin to spread the seeds. A rake was used to cover the seeds.

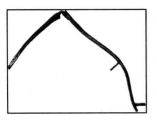

Scythe

When the grain was almost ripe it was cut with the scythe a long hooked blade fastened to a wooden handle. It was tied with a piece of straw into bundles twelve inches in diameter. A shock of harvested grain was constructed by standing the bundles up with the heads to the top. A field of shocked grain was a beautiful sight and satisfying, too. After the grain ripened it was taken to the shed where it was stored until they had time to thresh it. The storage shed was twenty-feet wide and sixty-feet long. The floor in this building was finished with the same manure texture that was used for the floor in the house. This kept the grain from falling into the cracks.

To begin the threshing process the heads were cut off and beaten with the thresher loosening the grain from the straw. The thresher was a leather strap in the form of a figure eight fastened to the end of the stick. The grain was put into a bucket or container and then they raised it above their head pouring slowly as a slight breeze blew through the open doors of the shed separating the grain from the straw. The grain was heavier than the straw so it fell in front of them while the breeze blew the chaff away. If the wind was too strong it also blew the grain. The grain was sifted many times to separate it from the straw. It was taken to the mill to be ground into flour. The mill owner took a portion of the grain for his services. The farmer took the remaining flour home to be used for breads, noodles, pastas and other foods. All the grain was used to feed the family. There was never enough to feed the livestock.

After the fields were cleared of the grain shocks, the cattle were allowed to graze in these fields to eat the loose straw and stubble.

Potatoes were planted in one field. Potatoes that were not consumed by the family were cooked and mashed into slop for the pigs that were going to be slaughtered for family consumption. The rest of the pigs received a meal of this potato slop once or twice a week. When the pigs weighed more than two hundred pounds they were butchered. Most families had only one cow, a calf, a heifer, four or five pigs and a team of oxen. The wealthiest family owned a bull and a boar that was rented to the villagers to breed their animals.

The women always did the milking. If she became ill or for some reason couldn't milk the cow a neighbor's wife did the milking because men never learned how.

The cattle pasture was wooded because the village was not far from the forest. The younger boys watched over the cattle and kept them confined to one area because there were no fences. There were also herdsmen for the pigs that were in a different pasture where the shrubbery was only three to six feet tall. The herdsmen received pay from the villagers for their services. A member of the family acted as herdsman to the oxen on Sundays. During the week these animals were used for farming.

3

One day, a bull began to paw the ground so Dad started imitating him. This made the bull angry and he charged after Dad forcing him to climb a tree. The bull stayed there watching Dad for the rest of the day; luckily the other boys could still herd the cows. At the end of the day an adult came to help Dad. He learned his lesson and never teased the bull again but it was too late because the bull now charged at anyone.

The families that had four to six chickens had them sleep in the kitchen under a portion of the stove during the winter. The families that could afford more chickens kept them in the section of the barn next to the kitchen providing them with heat. When the family had a "setting hen" they provided her with a private area behind the stove to allow her to nest on the fertile eggs that took twenty-one days to hatch. The only time she left the nest was to eat, drink and rid herself of waste. After the eggs hatched the baby chicks remained close to the nest until they had grown enough feathers to keep warm.

The villagers were quite resourceful and wasted little. The only fried pork eaten was pork chops. Everything else was baked or made into soup. The ham shank was cooked with dried beans. Vegetable soup was commonly made with pork or beef. Joints made the best soup. Noodles were almost always made for chicken soup. Even in the summer the family occasionally purchased a soup bone for Sunday lunch. Beef was never purchased for a weekday meal. They never purchased any pork or chicken. They ate all the chickens they didn't keep for laying eggs. As soon as the weather got cold enough for the temperature to stay below 40 degrees for several weeks, any family that had a beef to butcher did so at this time. Nature was their refrigerator.

They had very large gardens consisting of green beans, pinto beans, beets, carrots, cabbage, leaf lettuce, peas, dill, onions, parsley, garlic, cucumbers, kohlrabi, and sometimes watermelon. Kohlrabi is a wild cabbage that came from Northern Europe. It dates back to the 1600's. The Europeans were so tired of this vegetable that when they came to America and had other foods to eat they didn't introduce it to their children. The lack of demand makes it difficult to find in our stores today but it can be found in parts of Iowa. If you like cabbage or turnips you will like this vegetable.

Green beans were always eaten creamed. Cream and flour were made into a white sauce and poured over the cooked green beans. Brown gravy was prepared for lettuce by browning flour in a skillet and adding water and vinegar to taste.

Pickles were preserved in a barrel of salt water with dill. Enough salt was added to float a raw egg and then it was poured over the dill-sized pickles. The white film that formed on this brine preserved the pickles. When the pickles were eaten only a dozen or so were taken out at one time not disturbing the preserving film. Mother continued making this type of pickle even in America until she became acquainted with vinegar. Sauerkraut was one of the main winter foods used as a substitute for a vegetable.

Corn that was not eaten fresh was dried and made into yellow corn meal and eaten as corn meal-mush with fried butter. Fried butter was made by melting butter in a skillet and browned. They had to be careful not to let it burn.

*****

The villagers were very social. A common tradition was to greet visitors or relatives with a glass of wine, champagne or other spirits; even the small children were included. People would visit and sip the home brewed alcohol. Crystal glasses were commonly used because crystal was made in Czechoslovakia. To this day Czechoslovakia is known around the world for its crystal.

The Slovak people also love music. Dancing every Saturday in the villages was a big event. Mother told me, when young lads from other villages came to see if they could find a maiden the young men from my town would say, 'These are our girls. Go back to your own town.' Of course the young men still came. My mother's younger sister married a man from Poproc.

The Slovak people are quite talented and many can play musical instruments by ear. Unfortunately, in those days very few families could afford musical instruments for their children.

Another social activity throughout the year was visiting the cemetery. At the headstone people placed flowers and a container with a candle. All the available members of the family gathered around to commemorate the souls of the dead.

It was mandatory for all young men to enter the military service. That is why my father didn't marry until his late twenties. After Dad and Mom were married he had a chance to come to America. They referred to this country as "America" not the United States. Dad was in a caisson division serving in Russia, Germany and Pol-

and. While there he learned to speak all three languages as well as being proficient in his native Slovak tongue.

Dad said, "We made our decision to come to America because I had developed a friendship with some German soldiers who encouraged me. The Germans made arrangements for a group to depart from one of their ports so we decided to join them to fulfill our dreams." Dad and two of his brothers Uncle Mike, Uncle Steve and Mom's brother Uncle Joe pooled their hard earned money together to head for America.

New Beginnings: Living in Indiana

Mom and Dad were married July 13, 1902 in Rudnik, Austria-Hungary. Several months after the wedding Dad boarded the ship "Columbia" and departed from Hamburg, Germany, for America. He arrived on October 12, 1902 at Ellis Island. His first job was in a coal mine in Brownsville, Pennsylvania.

The coal mining companies had an agreement with foreign workers where the miners worked to pay their steamship fare and earned money for the wives' fare. It took Dad nearly two years to earn enough money before he could send for Mom. By that time John was about fifteen months old.

When Mom left her in-laws home in Rudnik she took one suitcase. Her relatives had given her some special things. One such item was seeds because my parents hoped to be farmers.

Mom walked with baby John to Kosice. She took the train to Bremen, Germany where she boarded a ship for the journey to the land of the free, and arrived at Ellis Island in the summer of 1904.

By then, Dad had moved to Indiana. Mom and John took a train to Terre Haute. From there it was thirty-one miles to Jasonville where Dad was working in a coal mine.

Dad's parents, John and Anna Kochis, my grandparents, came to America in 1905 and stayed with my parents until they moved to Colorado. John and Anna went back to Pennsylvania to stay with their daughter until 1911. Then they moved back to Europe and remained there for the rest of their lives.

The house in Indiana consisted of a kitchen and three bedrooms. My grandparents, parents, and John had one bedroom and six or eight men had the other two bedrooms. The other men were also working in the mines and lived there rent-free because the houses belonged to the mining companies. The married ones were saving money to send for their families. Mom earned money by doing the laundry, cooking, mending, ironing and other household duties for these men.

There was an oven made of stone beside the house. A fire was built inside the oven and when it was hot enough the ashes were removed and bread was placed in it to bake. A metal door kept the heat in while the bread was baking.

The neighbor women helped each other. They gave Mom the yeast culture for making bread, introduced her to tomatoes and taught her how to preserve food in jars. Mom had a small garden at her first home.

While in Indiana Mom had three more children, Kate, Andy and Paul. Andy died when he was several months old. They named the next baby Andy. Many years later Dad said to me, "The son we lost in Indiana was only slightly ill before he passed away." Now that I know about SIDS (Sudden Infant Death Syndrome) I am wondering if this is what happened to my baby brother. Since babies died of so many things in the early 1900's no one will ever know.

Dad did not like working in a coal mine so he applied for a job on the railroad where he built section houses and depots from Indiana to Colorado. The man that was responsible for maintaining the tracks was known as the section boss and entitled to live in the section house.

While living in Marshall, Colorado, Dad again worked in a coal mine while waiting for his rights from the government to move to a farm and homestead.

Citizenship paper

Moving to the Homestead

Dad had filed for citizenship in Brazil, Indiana on November 5, 1906. He became a citizen November 7, 1913 while living near Mattison, Colorado in Elbert County. Mattison was misspelled by the railroad. The correct spelling is Matheson and was changed a few years later.

9

Dad was 5'6" tall and weighed 165 pounds. Mom was 5'3" tall and weighed 140 pounds. In their golden years Dad gained to 185 pounds, but Mom was only 4'10" tall and weighed 125 pounds.

*****

The need to populate vast areas of the open West dictated an open-handed land policy by the Federal Government. The passage of the Homestead Act by Congress in 1862 was the culmination of more than seventy years of controversy over the disposition of public lands. From 1830 onward groups called for free distribution of such lands. This law transferred millions of acres to settlers, virtually free of charge. The Act, which became law on January 1, 1863 allowed anyone to file for a quarter section of free land (160 acres). At the end of five years the land belonged to them if they built on it, dug a well, plowed ten acres, fenced their land and actually lived there. Additionally one could claim a quarter section of land by "timber culture" (commonly called a "tree claim"). This required that they plant and successfully cultivate ten acres of timber.

If a homesteader left before five years anyone could take over and live on the land. This was called claim jumping, and happened frequently. Many farmers moved because the dry land in Eastern Colorado of 160 acres was not adequate to support a family. There was no water available for irrigation and the same is true today. There was an option to purchase the land after six months of residency for $1.25 per acre.

When the Federal Government undertook to survey the public lands they used a rectangular survey system that imposed a grid over the land. The units of measurements were "sections" composed of one square mile and therefore a section contains 640 acres. A township consists of thirty-six square sections and an acre from one of the sections was set aside for a public school.

When land passed from government ownership into the hands of an individual a document was issued to certify ownership. This document was called a land patent and was used by the individual to prove his ownership when he registered the deed with the appropriate county government office.

Dad filed for land under the Homestead Act. In the spring of 1908 the paperwork for was completed. The place was located four miles from Resolis. It was mapped out as a town and remains so to this day. There were six blocks in Resolis that included a water tower for the railroad, some cattle holding pens and a railroad section house. Resolis was ten miles west of Limon, Colorado towards Colorado Springs, Colorado on the Rock Island Railroad line.

My folks received their homestead in the same area were Dad's brothers, Uncle Mike and Uncle Steve each received 320 acres because they had the additional 160 acres of timber culture. Each of the three brothers lived on a different section.

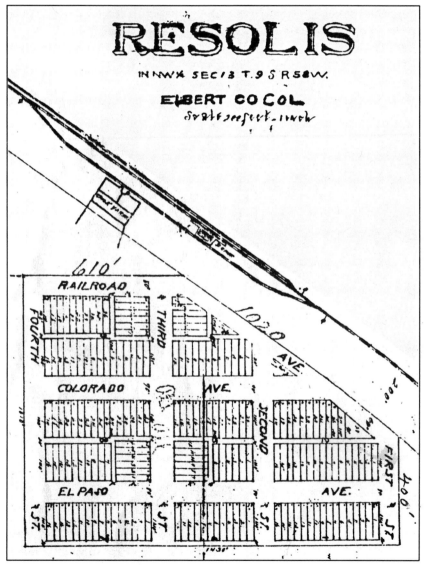

The first homes built were of sod that was easily accessible. Sod was plowed with a special shear that cut the soil just below the surface of the grass roots. The top part of the soil consisting of grass, roots and dirt was scraped off in sections 18 inches wide. This was layered as bricks are today. Even though the sod blocks were good insulating material there was no insulation in the ceiling so most of the heat was lost. In the winter people woke up with snow in the house.

Sod house in the background

Dad went to the homestead and built a one-room sod house that was fourteen feet square. When Dad completed the room Mom boarded a train with the three children and arrived at Resolis, Colorado. She walked the four miles to the homestead even though the railroad tracks came within one mile of the house. Mom helped Dad build another room fourteen feet square. The floor was finished with the same manure paste as in Europe. All the farm buildings on the homestead were of sod, except the hog house that was a cave dug in a hillside for the pigs. The homestead was four miles north and four miles east of Matheson, a small town sixty miles east of Colorado Springs on US Highway 24.

In those days living on the homestead took character, ingenuity and a lot of physical strength. The most important challenge was preserving food. They learned how to do with what they had living off the land. But like anything else some good comes with the bad. The bad was no electricity, refrigeration, running water or all night heat. The good was the good taste of homegrown chickens and meat without preservatives, homegrown garden vegetables and fruits not sprayed with pesticides or herbicides.

Cooperation and partnership describe the turn-of-the-century family farm. Marriage meant more than companionship and child bearing. It was a lifelong joint business venture. The farm needed the contribution of both women and men to exist.

Many financial problems existed. There was very little money. In the summer they farmed their land and during the winter months the men found work in the local coalmines, or the railroad, or wherever work existed. Most families had many children to help on the farms to grow their own food. Fortunately, crops yielded well in the virgin soil that was extremely rich in minerals but crop prices remained low because each family grew their own food so there was no market.

Mom directed and supervised the important parts of the farm. She along with us girls helped with the men's work whenever and wherever needed. Mom kept the farm accounts and made business decisions and taught us the things she knew about household duties. With Mom's supervision we grew and learned, collected and canned vegetables, butchered meat and processed everything we raised or grew and needed for our winter consumption.

Our farm had a diversified livestock population including cattle, pigs and poultry. Some farmers had sheep but the few we had were orphans that were given to us from the nearby Wells Ranch. We fed our crops to the animals and sold the stock and any surplus crops. For the most part the men worked out-of-doors producing raw agricultural materials to pay the mortgage, upgrade the stock or purchase more advanced farm equipment.

Mom's work centered on the home where we engaged in agricultural production of a different sort functioning as domestic workers. We produced goods for the household and sale. Our home served as the factory where we converted raw materials into products for the family.

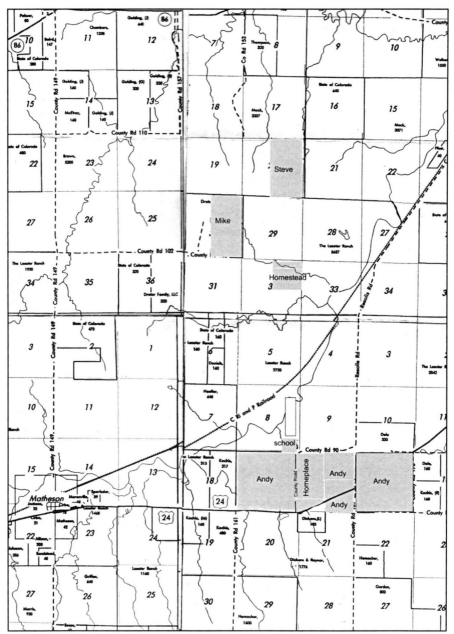

We earned cash income by raising chickens and selling eggs. We churned cream and sold butter and the excess cream. The cash income became an important and often vital part for the survival of the farm. In hard times when major farm crops failed to produce enough for sale, it was the cash that kept the folks from losing the farm.

There was a stream running through the homestead but my folks couldn't rely on water from it so they dug a well by hand using a shovel and a bucket to reach water. A well was mandatory in order to get a homestead grant. The first year crops on the homestead were corn, wheat, rye, potatoes and barley. Oats were added the second year and beans the third year.

Harrow

Mom and Dad started the homestead with one team of horses, a cow, a calf, a sow and a few chickens. The machinery they used at that time was a "plow," a "hayrack" and a "harrow."[1] It soon became necessary to purchase a "wagon box" for the purpose of hauling grain.[2] The wagon box and hayrack fit the same "chas-

Wagon Box

sis" so my folks had only one set of wheels for both pieces of equipment. While on the homestead Dad walked to Matheson to work on the railroad while Mom did the farming. She also drove the team of horses to the railroad to pick up the used railroad ties that she brought home for firewood. While at the tracks Mom and my siblings also picked

Wagon Box Chassis

up coal that had fallen off the cars. At first there were no reins to guide the horses. For a right hand turn the word "Gee" was shouted and the team would turn to the right. For them to turn to the left the word "Haw" was used.

A very common type of fuel for heat was cow-chips. Cow-chips are dried manure that lay out in the pasture. Mom and the children walked the pastures picking up cow chips, putting them in a sack and taking them home to burn. Duncan Matheson's son John described cow chips as "dried grass chewed up twice."

At one time Dad also worked at the Golden Cycle Mill in Colorado Springs. He was shoveling grain when the boss come over to him and said, "Mr. Kochis you are not working hard enough." Dad said, "If I am not working good enough for you, do it yourself." He took his shovel, stuck it into the grain and walked off the job.

There were no telephones in our rural area in those days, no insurance and no electricity. Therefore there were no monthly bills.

The early settlers faced many hardships. There were horrible winter blizzards, long summer droughts and dust storms, including the famous Dust Bowl days of the 1930s. There were hailstorms, diseases, financial problems and inefficient tools.

One of the most unpredictable hardships was a blizzard. Winter snowstorms could be so severe a person couldn't see far enough to walk safely from the house to the barn. Three-day blizzards making huge snowdrifts were common. During these blizzards the farmers tied a rope or wire between the house and the other buildings so they could find the way back to the house. Some farmers tied a rope around their waist and the door of the house so they could find their way back. One such snowstorm happened in December 1913. That was one of the worst storms on record in Eastern Colorado. The snow fell quietly for three days and nights covering the fence posts. This work of nature was beautiful but then it started to rain and the snow froze forming a crust. Then a blizzard came with more snow that lasted twenty-four hours. The rest of the winter people traveled on snowshoes and sleds. The local doctor in Matheson was forced to visit his patients on skis.

In the early 1950's we also began seeing tornadoes in the Matheson area. All Colorado weather was not bad. I tell of these blizzards, hail and dust storms so that you may understand some of the hardships the pioneers endured. There was also a lot of beautiful weather with moonlight shining on the snow. Winter fun included bundling up and going for a sleigh ride, sledding down the steep hills or ice-skating on the lagoons or ponds.

While on the homestead Uncle Mike married Aunt Anna and they had one child, Margaret. Leaving the homestead near Matheson, they moved to Aztec, New Mexico. Margaret had two boys and when she died Uncle Mike and Aunt Anna raised them.

In 1942 we received a telegram that Uncle Mike was killed in an auto accident between Farmington and Aztec. His funeral was to be held the next day. Andy was going to take Mom and Dad to the funeral so after the chores were done I proceeded to gas up the car and get it ready for the trip. After starting the car I went to move it and the lights went out. Now what? Mom and I tied a gasoline lantern to the front of the car and went to John's house. He lived on the highway three miles west of us. I couldn't go very fast because the wind dimmed the light from the lantern and I couldn't see. John couldn't find a short but when I stepped on the clutch it blew a fuse putting out the lights. He told me to go to Andy's and maybe he could find the short but every time I pushed in the clutch to shift gears I had to shut off the lights. Andy found a frayed wire and when I stepped on the clutch it touched that wire causing a short and burned a fuse. He fixed it.

We were getting close to the turn off of U.S. Highway 24 when a car came up behind us. Mom asked me to pull over and let the other car pass but I had already rolled down my window and extended my arm signaling that I wanted to make a left hand turn. (There were no turning signals on cars in those days.) The car also turned coming down the road following us. That was strange because it was after 10:00 pm. Still stranger yet was that the car followed us into our yard. It was none other than Aunt Mary (Mom's sister) and three of her daughters from Durango. Mom wanted to visit with her sister and they also wanted to attend the funeral. The girls and I went into Matheson and called Aunt Anna (Uncle Mike's wife) asking her to postpone the funeral so everyone could attend and she did.

Tragedy struck Uncle Steve in 1912 when he lost his wife Aunt Mary. Kate told me, "Aunt Mary died when Albert was born." There were no nursing bottles at that time so Mom took over breast-feeding the baby until he was six months old. She also helped the oldest girl of eleven to care for all her siblings and taught her what she needed to know about running a household. A lot of women lost their lives at that time because almost all the babies were born at home with only midwives to help instead of doctors. If a woman got an infection and started to hemorrhage or any of the other birthing problems, they didn't know what to do. Pacifiers were made by putting sugar in a small square piece of cloth and tying the corners holding the sugar called a "sugar teat."

Uncle Steve sold his homestead and purchased land four miles north of Calhan, Colorado but hadn't had the opportunity to move. When Aunt Mary died Uncle Steve sent a telegram to his friend Bob in Calhan saying, "I am sending my wife to you on the train," but failed to tell Bob that his wife had died. Bob took his buggy and went to meet the train but was shocked to see the employees unloading a coffin. He had to go back home and get a wagon.

In those days the bodies were dressed at home and never cremated. The neighbor ladies didn't let Mother help to dress Aunt Mary because Mom was pregnant and they believed it was not good for a pregnant woman to care for the dead.

Uncle Steve later married a widowed mail order bride from Pennsylvania who left her four young sons there. Aunt Lizzy sent for her youngest son when he was maybe seven or eight years old. He was afraid he was coming to the Wild West and would encounter Indians. Later two of her children moved to Colorado but one stayed in Pennsylvania.

Uncle Steve built his house with three rooms in a row. The kitchen was on the north end. One day lightening struck the house on the south side and shattered one of the doors that was closed between two rooms. Three of the children were leaning against the stove. Had that door not been closed lightening would have killed all three.

Home at Last: The Homeplace

In 1916 after eight years the folks sold the homestead of 160 acres. They bought 320 acres on the plains four miles east of Matheson. We fondly call it the "Home Place."

Having water for the livestock and the house was the first thing Dad did on the Home Place. In those days there was no well drilling equipment. All water wells were dug by hand. It makes me wonder what kind of soil it was. It was sandy on the surface.

Dad found water a quarter of a mile south of the northwest corner of the property. The well was forty feet deep. The water table was four feet above the bottom. An underground spring fed the well. It was never pumped dry. The water level didn't drop. After many years the pipes just above the water line sprang a leak and sprayed water on the walls washing soil into the well. We had no water. John owned a well drilling rig. It had a suction bucket that was made from heavy metal and was five feet long and twelve inches in diameter. My brothers cleaned out the mud. As it was dropped in the well it filled with sand. When we started to lift it out a valve on the bottom went shut. When we pulled it up it was full of soil. I was standing on top of the cooler holding a mirror so the sun could reflect down into the well so they could see what they were doing. George and Helen brought a piece of smoke stack pipe from the steel mill and we scrubbed it out and put it down the well and that made a good casing. When the folks left in 1961 they were still using the well.

Many wells were over one-hundred-fifty-feet deep. They plastered or bricked them on their way down to keep the well from caving. How they ever hand dug them I have no idea because when a lantern was lowered down it went out. That was a sign there was no oxygen.

While Dad was digging the hole for the well Mother was pulling the full containers of dirt out hand over hand, meantime looking after the children. Mother said, "Dad dug in two or three different places before finding water. He always stopped short of finding water and I could never convince him to dig a little deeper." Apparently Dad didn't use a witching person to find water. Witching for water required a special talent. The person doing the witching used a twig or branch from a tree but willow was the best. The twig needed to be in the shape of a wishbone. The person doing the witching held the branch with the tip pointing up. As the person began to approach water the twig started to turn and they marked the spot. When the twig was pointing down that meant they were over water. They measured from the spot where the twig started to turn down to where they were standing meant it was that many feet to water. Some people are better at witching than others. One farmer didn't believe this and accused the person carrying the twig of just letting it turn down as they walked. This made the person so angry he took the twig and held it so tight that his fingernails cut the bark from the twig as they witched for water. After seeing the bark being ripped from the twig the farmer became a believer.

Bucket and pulley for drawing water

Initially the water was drawn with a bucket hand over hand. Later a pulley was used for several years before my folks erected a metal stand for their windmill. (Most stands were made of wood.)

The farm buildings were on the side of a hill with the barn on the top and the house and well on the lower side. I'm sure they never thought of sanitation but no one was seriously ill from drinking the water.

After the well was dug they started building the farm buildings and the house. The front of the house faced the west with a view of the Rocky Mountains seventy miles away.[3] The man who plastered the Antler's hotel in Colorado Springs plastered our house. (The hotel became a famous landmark, but is now the Double Tree Hotel.)

The first morning on the job the man asked "Who is going to mix the mud for me?"

"My boys and me," John was thirteen and Paul was ten.

The man looked at Dad and my brothers and said, "Do you think for one minute that you and those children can do the job? You are off your rocker. Forget it."

"I hired you to plaster the walls not mix the mud."

After several hours of working, they took a break. While resting the man said to Dad, "Mr. Kochis, I am sorry for what I said this morning about you and the boys. I wish you and your boys mixed plaster for me every day. This is the best mud I have ever used. Usually it is too thin, too thick, or already set. The men who mixed plaster for me at the Antlers Hotel stood around instead of working."

Even though no one has lived in the house since 1965, I noticed the plaster was still on the walls in March 1974. There were just a few small cracks that had formed and were there when I was young.

Home Place

Building up the Homeplace

The first buildings built on the farm were all wood framed. The first barn was made of 1x12s placed in a vertical position with lathes over the cracks to keep out the wind and snow. Later it was covered with tin. This barn held eight horses in stalls and included a hayloft. It was also used as a milk barn. There were some chains fastened to the trough and then around the cow's neck but this allowed the cow too much freedom for milking. An addition was built on the north side with stanchions. Stanchions were a device where a cow's head is locked in between a set of 2x4s for milking. Grain is fed to the cow while she waits. On the other side of the barn another section was built as a holding pen. A space from the hayloft was opened to drop feed down into a trough to feed the cattle during bad weather.

A "brooder house," was built for the purpose of housing baby turkeys. In the summer when there were bad storms the turkeys become frightened very easily and flew out into the storm and perished rather than stay under shelter. Turkeys were hard birds to raise but were a good source of income. I would call them half-wild because they roamed away from the farm buildings. That made them prey for the coyote. When the coyotes became over populated and came close to the farm buildings they would attack in broad daylight. When it was no longer profitable to raise turkeys, Mom used the brooder house for her first setting hens of the season and for the young chickens.

On nice days mother gave the younger children the task of stripping the fine fluff off the feathers from the quill so she could make softer pillows. Mom took the wing or tail feathers from chickens or turkeys and made a pastry brush. She used three or four and tied the stems together. The feather pastry brush didn't lose bristles after it got old.

Within the next year after starting the new farm my folks built a silo of bricks for ensilage. This was a cinder type material sixteen inches square with three holes in the center. The bricks were only one inch thick and the holes inside were three inches square.

All the buildings had lap siding and were painted brown with white trim. A chicken house and garage was built with a mutual wall. The garage had a workbench in the back and along one side. Fifty-five gallon gas barrels occupied the chicken house side and both had southern entrances. We filled these barrels with gas for the car and tractor. In the chicken house on the south side were nests for the hens to lay eggs. On the other side were roosts that are perches for fowl to wrap their claws around when they sleep. The roosts in our chicken house were ladder types. As the chicken flock increased more roosts were needed. The boys replaced the ladders by building a platform two thirds of the way from the back. A foot above the platform they placed 2x2s separated far enough apart for the chickens to roost comfortably. When it came time to clean the chicken house we removed the 2x2s.

When my folks built the chicken house they made eight pigeon nests on the east side for wild pigeons. As the pigeons multiplied we trapped them and had squab. I remember doing this once because those pigeons were hard to catch. The cats had their share of the young ones that would fall out of the nest before they learned to fly. The pigeons carried bed bugs and as the bugs got into the chicken house we got them on our clothes and carried them into the house. To keep the bed bugs down we took old motor oil with turpentine and spread it in the chicken house painting the platform and walls.

We had to paint the house to kill the bedbugs. To do so, we loosened the baseboard and painted with an oil base paint using turpentine for a thinner. The painting had to be done in the summer because the odor was so strong the windows had to be left open so we could breathe.

In those days a cellar was very important to families. There was neither electricity nor refrigerators to keep food from spoiling. A hole was dug into the ground eight feet wide by ten feet long for the cellar. The top was covered with planks and then with dirt for coolness in the summer and warmth in the winter. There was a door at the bottom that we just pulled shut and fastened to the post. A door was flat across the top to keep out the sun, cold, rain and snow. Later we built a granary with a root cellar under it closer to the house and used the old one for ice. Dirt was put around the exposed foundation of the granary where the cellar was above the ground. This insulated the cellar to keep things from freezing when it got too cold. Sometimes a coal-oil heater was put in the cellar. This also was where the sauerkraut, hams, bacon, sausage, and all home canned goods were kept as well as potatoes and garden vegetables. The granary above had wide doors on the other side from where we entered

Coal Oil Heater

the cellar. A trap door was built in the floor of the granary to lower potatoes down into the cellar. This was easier than carrying them down the steps to the back of the cellar. Boards were propped against the posts that were holding up the granary to keep the potatoes confined to the back so they didn't roll all over. Coal was stored in the cellar because the coal mined around the Matheson area was lignite. This is a soft coal that crumbles if left in the light.

The Barker mine was one mile south and the farmers helped free of charge to mine the coal when they went after a load. When farmers became too busy to help mine the coal it couldn't afford to stay open. There was too much rock in the coal for the mine to be profitable. There was another mine three miles west of the Barker mine and it remained open for a number of years because the coal was of a better quality. The coalmines on the plains eventually closed.

The lumberyards used to sell coal until people started using propane gas for heat. They not only handled lumber and coal but sold items of all types such as kitchen utensils, cream cans, milk buckets, coal-oil lamps and lanterns, the chimneys for them, block and tackle and the ropes, harnesses and the things used for pulling farm machinery. They sold anything we needed for the farm. Eventually the Mom and Pop stores in the small towns closed their doors. The older people passed away and the younger people moved to the cities. Fewer supplies were needed.

Let's go to the Barn Dance

The last building built on the home place was in 1927, the year I was born. It was a tile barn with a hayloft. They used the same type of tile as was used in the silo. My folks held "barn dances" on Saturday nights in the hayloft. The local people formed a musical group that played from 9:00 p.m. until 2:00 a.m. with a half hour break at midnight. Sometimes live music was not available, so my brothers took the phonograph and records up into the hayloft so the people could dance. During the thirty-minute break, snacks were served. Every one brought sandwiches or cookies. A big enamel coffee pot was used to boil the coffee.

There was also a five-gallon can of water in the hayloft and a dipper that hung on a nail by the can. When someone wanted a drink they dipped the dipper in the can, took out some water and drank from the dipper. If they didn't drink all the water they poured it back into the can or they handed it to the next person in line and that person finished the water. No one was ever concerned about transmittable diseases.

The roof of the barn was built in an "A" shape. If the men danced too close to the sides they hit their heads on the rafters. Women didn't bump their heads because they were not as tall. Little, big, young and old joined in the fun. When the little ones got tired they went to sleep on quilts in a corner of the hayloft. While these dances were going on, I was asleep but my older siblings were having a great time. Before we built the barn, dances were often held at a friend's house. The furniture would be moved out of one or two rooms and the rug rolled up. The barn dances were great fun because there was so much more room in the hayloft. Sometimes when it was too far for people to go home in the horse and buggy days, they stayed the night and went home early the next morning to do their chores.

When my sister Ann came home from Denver on some weekends she showed us some of the dances they did there. I learned some of the steps but not enough to do a complete dance. One was the Scottish, two others were the Charleston and the Cha-Cha-Cha. One had a special step where you slid your feet sideways to the song "Comin' Through The Rye."

I learned the dance "put your little foot" but I didn't have the opportunity to dance it because no one else had learned how. A few did the Mexican Hat Dance. Mostly we did the fox trot, two-step, waltz, polka and western square dances. I still have a box of cards with the words for calling square dances. Later the bunny hop became very popular.

Brothers Frank and Steve liked to tease the girls when they were at the dances. We had a toffee candy called kisses wrapped in paper twisted on both ends. They put some in their pockets and while standing around the dance floor with their hands in their pockets, they asked a girl, "Would you like a kiss?"

The girl would say, "No."

The brother who asked the question took his hands out of his pockets and holding the piece of candy by both ends would say, "Fine, I'll eat it myself."

The girl grabbed the candy saying, "Oh! I'll have that type of kiss!"

On Sunday afternoons we had guests, so after lunch my folks danced in the kitchen because it was the largest room in the house and it was easy to push the table to the side. They used the phonograph and records for music.

When I was a teenager I went with my older siblings to dances at places such as church halls, American Legion buildings or some other large building or haylofts owned by friends and neighbors. The men were charged twenty-five cents and entry for the ladies was free. Sodas cost a dime. When I dated we attended these types of dances on Saturday nights.

Building a Fence with Wooden Posts

Replacing a broken post took two people to dig the part out of the ground. Using a spade shovel and a crowbar we hooked these tools into the broken post and pried it out by pushing down on the spade and crowbar. This enabled us to get the broken piece of post out for firewood. The new hole needed to be at least two feet deep to stabilize the

Wooden fence posts

post securely. When putting up a new fence we used a crow bar to loosen the hard soil and then dig the hole with the spade shovel.[4] Later we got a posthole digger that had two shovels and two handles that worked like a pair of scissors. Holding the handles we shoved it into the loose dirt, then opening the handles we brought a shovel full of dirt from the hole. Later a post-

Post hole driller

hole digger was invented that looked like an auger that fastened onto the tractor and was driven by the power take off shaft.[5] When the hole was deep enough we cleaned the loose dirt from the hole and set the post.

When we were putting up new fence or repairing the old one, a wire stretcher was used. There was a clasp on both ends with a chain on one

Hydraulic Post hold driller

end to fasten around the post. For repairs we put the wire in both clasps tightening the wire and holding it while repairs were made. The wire stretcher was a two-and-a-half foot long bar, two inches wide with cogs in it and a handle. We moved the handle back and forth and when it caught

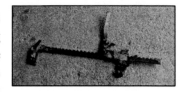

Wire stretcher

in these cogs it stretched the wire. To hold the wire on the post we used a staple. These varied from one-and-a-half to two inches long. When a farmer purchased land adjacent to his, he sometimes needed a gate in the middle. Instead of stapling the wire to the post we drove two staples horizontally in the post and put the wire between the staples and dropped another staple on the outside of the wire to hold it in place. This was done for several posts. When the gate was needed all we had to do was lift out the staples and remove the wire. We put it on the ground and went through. There were no steel posts then and on some country roads you might still see wooden posts.

By the mid-30's steel posts became very popular because they were so easy to set. The State highway department used steel posts for corners and gates and cemented them in place. We still used wooden posts. Steel posts required cement to hold them in place; what was left over would get hard and be wasted.

Bypassing the Horse Shoe Curve:
Name Change of Roads in 1929

There was a steep hill three fourths mile south and three-fourths mile east of the house. The road curved like a mountain highway. We called it "The Horseshoe Curve" and it consisted of four acres. John and Paul pastured cattle in this curve on days when they were free of fieldwork. One day while the boys were acting as herdsmen they saw a pasteboard box. They were full of mischief so when a short time later they saw a snake, Paul ran back to get the box while John kept an eye on the snake. They captured the snake, put it in the box, put it in the middle of the highway and waited patiently for the first car. There was little traffic in those days and the average speed was twenty to twenty-five miles per hour so it was quite some time before a car came. The first one drove past but the next car stopped, picked up the box and drove off without looking inside. Those two boys laughed until their sides hurt.

There were no signs alerting traffic of the upcoming horseshoe curve. The cars traveled so slowly it was easy for the driver to see the dangerous curve in the daytime. After dark they lost control and wrecked but rarely was anyone hurt so they waited until daylight to get help. Our farm was visible from the curve so they walked to our place. We had no telephone but one of my brothers drove them into town to report the accident and get help.

Counties owned the roads until December 31, 1928. The highway east of Limon that is now U. S. Highway 24 was called North Highway 40. U. S. Highway 40 west of Limon was called South Highway 40. The highway with the horseshoe curve from Limon to Colorado Springs was North Highway 40 and the road from Limon to Denver was South Highway 40. This was confusing. In January 1929 the state took ownership, fired the county employees and hired new men changing South Highway 40 to U.S. Highway 40, and North Highway 40 to U.S. Highway 24.

When the names of the highways were changed the state started to blacktop U.S Highway 24 beginning in Colorado Springs. In the mid 1930's they were in our area and re-routed the road with plans to go through two sections of our land. My folks refused them access because the State did not want to hire my brothers, our horses, wagons and other equipment. When the State agreed to these conditions, my brothers had a job with the state and the highway went through our land.

Fresno Scraper

The highways were built with horses and a large scoop called a "Fresno Scraper" pulled by six head of horses.[6]

The Fresno Scraper moved the dirt where it was needed similar to how a bulldozer or front-end loader does today. When building U.S. Highway 24 my brothers also used a plow to loosen the soil. Our wagon box was used to haul the steel posts and the boys drove them into the ground with a sledgehammer.[7] Today farmers use steel posts and a steel post driver. When U. S. Highway 24 was built and they bypassed the horseshoe curve the road was one half mile long. They filled in the low spot leaving a high embankment. One day some tourists were going to Colorado Springs to a funeral and lost control of their car rolling over three times. All three passengers were thrown from the car and killed.

Steel post driver

Sledge hammer

Working with Smart Horses

Horses or oxen pulled equipment before tractors were invented. There was no tongue or wheels on the hand-held plow, harrow or cultivator. This was hard work. The person guiding the equipment pulled it around as needed.

When one horse was used in a buggy there were two wooden tongues one on each side of the animal. A "singletree" was a wooden device fastened to the harness behind the animal enabling it to pull the cargo. As the driver guided the horse these wooden tongues were fastened to make the wheels turn to the side having the buggy follow. When a team is used the tongue is between the horses being held up with a "neck yoke" that kept the horses from hitting their legs when turning a corner. The tongue guided the wheels and a 2x6 four feet long with two singletrees fastened to each end makes a "double tree" and is used for a team.

Single Tree

Neck Yoke and Double Tree

Actually horses do not pull. They push with their shoulders. When horses are in front of the piece of machinery they were really pushing but we say they are pulling because the wagon or piece of machinery is behind them. Each horse has a special collar that goes around his neck, a "horse collar" that is part of the "harness" enabling him to push. If these collars don't fit correctly the horse will get a sore on his shoulder and be unable to work. Each horse is unique and a different size.

A "hayrack" was eight feet wide and twelve feet long. It was used for

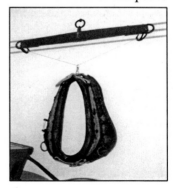

Single Tree and Horse collar

hauling feed, bundles, and large loads. There were no roads and far-mers cut across pastures taking the shortest distance.[8] When gravel roads were built manufacturers made steel wheels two and a half feet in diameter and four inches wide. The wood and steel wheels made for rough riding, shaking the cargo because there were no springs on the axles. As the years went by my brothers got some rims from cars. They cut the steel rims from the wagon wheels in just the right place to fit inside the car rims. The local blacksmith welded the wheels to the car rims. Using rubber tires that were still good, they mounted them on the wagon wheels. The first rubber tires had inner tubes. If we had a flat tire we had to disassemble it, take the tube out and patch it.[9]

Drive Belt and Hayrack

Branding: Cattle Drives:
Railroad: Small Towns

Since the 1860's brands have been burned into a calf's hide to prove ownership. Cattle were branded with a branding iron. The State Branding Board deals with ownership disputes. Today fourteen states have brand inspectors, most of them in the west. These people are licensed peace officers and are authorized to carry guns. Twenty states have theft investigators who cover both livestock thefts and stolen agricultural property. The only state that requires all cattle to be branded is New Mexico where unbranded cattle "over weaning age" legally belong to the state.

The Colorado Brand Board became a state agency in 1903. Every existing brand with its description and list of current and previous owners and other information is located in the Brand Boards central office and has been housed in the historic Stock Exchange building in Denver since 1917.

Today, cattle rustling isn't as bad as it used to be but the wars between sheep and cattlemen men are still a problem. Rustling is easier today because they carry portable panels and loading chutes with them. If the gates to the pastures are locked they cut the wires and drive in with their trucks. They put the panels close to the herd, round up the cattle, place the chute up to the trucks, load the cattle and drive off. Colorado is still considered one of the most aggressive states when it comes to controlling livestock movement. By law, brand inspectors must certify papers and brands whenever a cow or horse is moved more than seventy-five miles within the state, is shipped out of state, ownership is changed or the animal is to be slaughtered. An experienced eye can tell at a glance and confirm that the brand matches the owner in possession of that animal.

In the 1860's new brand inspectors were first issued a pair of hand clippers (to clip the hair over the brand) a rope, a clipboard and a brand book. Today they still issue the same four items. It is getting increasingly difficult to find competent replacements for brand inspectors. The number of inspectors that responded to the last appeal was seventy. Only thirty-five arrived and twenty passed the qualifying written examination. All twenty failed the practical field test, which required them to identify brands on fifteen carefully selected head of cattle within ten minutes. Very few dairy cattle are branded because they are kept closer to home.

The branding board requires cattle ranchers and farmers to have three pieces in their branding irons. This made it harder for the rustlers to change the brands. Sometimes thieves owned several brands so they could put one of their brands over the existing one.

My folks' "branding iron" was two pieces: an upside down "Y" with the shape of a heart upside down under the "Y". A two-piece branding iron is considered an antique today and cannot be purchased. It must be registered and kept up to date to be of any value. We had a branding chute to use when we were working on our cattle but never branded any of them.[10] I do remember seeing the brand on some of the older cattle.

Branding chute

Before the railroads were built the ranchers had cattle drives. Cattle were branded to prove ownership at the end of the drives. The ranchers rounded up all the livestock they wanted to take to market and drove them all the way to a slaughterhouse or where there was a major railroad yard to ship them the rest of the way. These drives were time consuming as they only traveled ten miles in a day. Cattle drives were operated by a trail boss who was familiar with the terrain and weather for that part of the country where they were to travel. He knew where there was water. The leader would oversee to all the needs of the people and cattle. There were two chuck wagons on the drives. One carried the cooking utensils and the other carried the food. Livestock lost weight on these drives because they did not have time to eat. Many animals were lost because of stampedes, wild animals, storms, thieves and many other mishaps that were encountered. Ranchers were relieved to see more railroads come to the west.

With the railroads came small towns that were built up in their wake. In these small towns there were "Stock Yards" consisting of corrals that held the livestock the farmers wanted to ship to market and a scale because the rail road company needed to know how much weight the train was pulling and how much to charge for freight. The rancher needed to order a railroad car made for livestock when he was ready to ship cattle.

Have you ever looked on a large-scale map and wondered why there was a town every ten or twelve miles? First, the trains needed water. Also this gave the farmer the opportunity to get the supplies he needed and get back home in one day. These small grocery stores had a post office. There was a bank at each of these towns but more than seventy-five-percent went broke during the depression in the 1930's.

The first locomotives used steam for power and needed water that was heated with coal. Usually they could only go ten to twelve miles on the open plains before they needed to refill their water tanks. The Rock Island Railroad ran from Limon to Colorado Springs. The first stop was Resolis ten miles west of Limon and the next stop was Ramah, twenty more miles west. The railroad asked a man by the name of Duncan Matheson to let them put a water tower on his land but he refused to give them the permission so they put up a tower at Simla. They found that it was still too far for the train to make the run. Mr. Matheson finally let them put up a water tower on his ranch thus starting the town of Matheson.

In those days travel was with horses so it took a long time to get to town and back home so in 1906 Mr. Matheson built a grocery store. At the Matheson Mercantile you could buy groceries, clothing, material, needles, thread, pins, linens, blankets, pots and pans, salt for the livestock, gas, hardware and even tractors. We sold our eggs to the grocery store for ten cents a dozen in exchange for the things we needed. Hot dogs came in large quantities and the storeowner weighed out how many we needed. Bologna was in one long tube and the clerk would cut off how much we wanted. If we wanted it sliced they charged extra. Longhorn cheese is the only kind of cheese they carried. It was in a large roll twelve inches in diameter and eighteen inches long. The clerk sliced so much he could guess very closely to a pound how much to slice.

By 1920 Matheson became a nice town with a bank, newspaper, grain elevator, three hotels, lumberyard, post office and several garages that repaired cars and sold gas. There was also a creamery that bought our cream then shipped it to the larger towns to be made into butter.

Some of the rural towns had a telephone office owned by private individuals. They owned the telephone lines, and the offices were in their homes. The wives were the switchboard operators and the husbands maintained the lines.

To make a call, a crank was turned on the home phone that rang into the switchboard. Matheson had electricity but they had a crank on the switchboard to use for backup in case of a power outage. When making a long distance call, the operator called Limon, who in turn transferred the call to switchboards in Colorado Springs or Denver. When lines were available these operators completed the call to the intended party. Many times it took all day to make a long distance call. When the call came through, the operator at Matheson called the party back that placed the call.

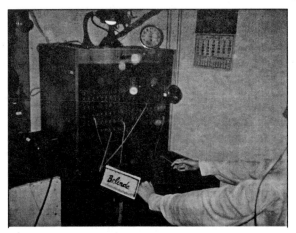

Telephone switchboard

In those days the rural phones were on "party lines". There could be as many as ten or more homes on one line.

Each home had a different number of rings to indicate who was being called. These consisted of a series of "long" and "short" rings.

If there was an emergency, like a house or grass fire, the switch board operator had a special set of rings. When these were heard everyone picked up the receiver to get the news. They dropped whatever they were doing and ran to help the neighbor.

Getting Virgin Soil Ready for Planting: New Machinery

When the soil was virgin it was very rich in nutrients and produced crops in abundance. My folks plowed up fifteen acres of sod when they first moved onto the home place. In that small space they grew enough feed for all the livestock they brought from the homestead and more than enough potatoes for the family and the pigs. Dad dug the rows with the walking plow and we walked in these furrows dropping the potato pieces eighteen inches apart. Mom made sure there was an "eye" in each piece as she cut the potatoes.

Throughout the year we put potatoes into a five-gallon metal bucket on the stove to cook for the pigs. We still had potatoes left from the previous season so before harvest time we fed them to the cows. Mother had us children cut them into small pieces so they didn't choke.

The soil was so nutritious they not only grew enough feed for the livestock and the family they even planted watermelons in the field. Mom said, "Our watermelons were nice and big, almost ready to eat when someone went in the field and plugged all the nice larger ones and turned the plug side down." Plugging a watermelon causes it to rot. To plug a watermelon to see if it is ripe a sharp knife is used cutting a triangle two inches each way and deep enough to get into the meat of the watermelon. We wondered if someone was looking for a good watermelon or doing this for spite. After they found the first few to be green they should have known all the rest would still be green.

The first pieces of equipment used on the farm was the "walking plow" that went eight inches into the ground moving the dirt to one side. It was called a walking plow because it was guided with two handles

Walking plow

while we walked behind a team of horses.

After larger equipment was introduced the walking plow was used to prepare our garden for planting and in the field when we planted potatoes.

Since the plows covered a small area the manufacturers made "disks." The disks varied in size but most were twelve inches in diameter and were sharp turning the soil to kill the weeds. Half of the disk put the soil to the right and the other half put it back to the left. When turning corners while pulling machinery it left some unturned soil because it didn't

Disk

follow the tractor tracks. When we finished the field we went up and down the corners the disk left unturned. The tractor that pulled the two-bottom plow could pull a twelve-foot disk since the disk only

went three inches into the ground. We covered more ground in less time but the disk didn't always get the weeds so the manufacturers came out with a "tandem" disk. This was one disk behind the other. The front part would put the soil one way to the outside and the back part turned it back to the inside getting the weeds the single disk missed.

Tandem disk

The next farm machine built was the "one-way." The disks on the one-way were larger and heavier being twenty-four inches in diameter. It had only one group of disks and put the soil one-way thus its name. It did a better job than the tandem disk because it went deeper. It was so wide we couldn't go through the gates so we pulled out a large pin like a smooth bolt that let the one-way drop back to

Oneway

be as wide as the tractor. This also was how we went down the road. When we got to the field all we did was back up just enough to line up the holes and drop in the pin.

The next piece of machinery the manufactures introduced was the "Grame-Hoeme." Hoeme is the name of the inventor. This piece of equipment had shanks sweeps. The sweeps were slightly pointed in a "V" shape and went just deep enough to cut the roots from the weeds. This didn't disturb the top of the soil as much therefore preventing the wind from blowing it away. These were the kinds of machinery used over the years in preparation for getting the soil ready for planting.

In the mean time the farmers still plowed the fields so manufacturers invented a larger plow. After we purchased a tractor to pull the larger pieces of machinery we got a "two-bottom" plow. This meant there were two plows one in front of the other. This was necessary for the soil of the second plow to fall into the furrow that was made by the first plow. As tractors became larger and stronger we got a "three-bottom" plow

Later the manufacturers made a "four-bottom" plow with four bottoms upside down. The upside down plows put the dirt to the left and when the farmer got to the end he used the hydraulic lift and the upside down plow turned over and put the dirt to the right. This allowed a farmer to turn around and come back down the field. He didn't have to go around not doing anything at the end of the fields. We did not invest in this plow.

One day the boys were going out to the field with a disk. Frank opened the gate and when Andy went through he didn't watch and the last disk ran over Frank's foot. Luckily there was a soap weed that a part of the disk ran over and saved

Two bottom plow

Frank's foot. As the disk ran over the soap weed it was lifted up keeping the disk from cutting deeper into his shoe and foot. The folks did not take Frank to the doctor. Mom poured peroxide on his foot and used a paste made with ground flax seed mixed with milk. She watched it closely and changed the bandage twice a day.

Planting Crops Gets Easier:
Cultivating vs Red Ants

Drill

At first, grain was planted by "broadcasting" just as my folks did in Czechoslovakia. As soon as they were available folks purchased a "Grain Drill" that operated on the same principal as the planter or lister, except the grain was poured into a carrier fifteen inches wide and as long as the drill.[11] As the tractors were invented and became bigger all the machinery was made larger allowing us to cover more ground in less time. When my folks' started to farm everything was done by hand and they were lucky to take care of one acre in several days. Today, huge implements are capable of covering hundreds of acres in one day.

Corn and beans were planted with the hoe after the ground was prepared with the walking plow. To plant corn a hole was dug and two or three kernels of corn were dropped in and then covered. Beans were planted in a row because they were planted closer together.

The first invention for planting was called a "two-row plan-

Two row planter

ter" that was pulled by a team. Above each row was a planter box holding the seeds. A flat disk that was operated in the planter box dropped a seed a certain distance from the last one enabling the planting to be done evenly.[12] The disk for beans had more holes than the one for corn. Seeds needed to be flat to go through the holes so Dad removed the round kernels from the end of the cobs and gave the rest to us to remove

by hand. They soon bought a "corn sheller" that we turned by hand. We dropped
one cob through at a time making it easier
on the hands. As we turned the crank the
solid wheel had spikes that spun the ear removing the corn. The corn dropped into a
bucket under the sheller. The cobs came out
of the end into a basket or tub.

Corn Sheller

The planter didn't put much soil
around the root of the corn so as it grew
taller the wind knocked it onto the ground
pulling out the roots. We had to pack dirt
around the stalk by hand. The work was more pleasant when a company invented a "two-row lister" pulled by six or more horses. This
made a deep ditch that enabled us to put more soil around the root to
keep the wind from blowing the corn over. The lister had shears like
a plow throwing the soil both ways making a deep furrow. Corn and
beans were the only large kernel crop we planted, the rest were small
grains and drilled.

As the tractors became larger so did the machinery. The farm
machine manufacturers became more knowledgeable as time went
by and someone invented the "four row lister" that fastened to the
side of the tractor. When we
got to the end of the row
there was a hydraulic lift
that raised the complete
piece of machinery from the
ground. There was a cultivator that fastened to the tractor in the same fashion.

Once the planting was
finished we tackled the weeds
with a little "hand held cultivator" pulled by one horse
between the rows of corn,

Hand held cultivator

beans, potatoes and watermelon. We weeded between the plants with
the hoe. When the larger cultivators were available the hand held cultivator was used in our garden. Later a larger "cultivator" was made to
coincide with the listed rows. There was a shield six inches high and

43

three inches on each side of the plants that protected the delicate crops while shears killed the tiny weeds along the listed ridges and put a small amount of soil by the plants. When the soil fell in between the plants it covered any weeds in the row, smothering them.

Cultivator

In the next cultivating period the shields were removed so more soil could fall against the plants making the roots even sturdier. The third time the banks were flattened so during harvest time the fields were level allowing the other machinery to run smoothly down the field.

*****

One day Helen and Mary were using the hand held cultivator in the garden. Mary was leading the horse so he wouldn't trample the small plants because she was not strong enough to handle the cultivator, and the rows were short.

In the field the rows were long so it was easier for the horses to know where to walk. We used to think a mule with its small feet would be preferable in the garden so it wouldn't step on the delicate plants. This was not true. We owned a huge horse named Shaddy, a black Percheron weighing a ton and his feet were huge but he didn't step on any plants. When we stopped he stood still and if he had to kick at a fly his foot came right back down under him not to the side. We never needed to put horseshoes on our horses because the soil was soft.

One hot day Mother brought the girls something to drink. They did not realize where they had stopped and Helen was standing in a red anthill. All of a sudden ants were biting her. The garden was by the road but the ants were pinching Helen so badly she started pulling off her clothes. Thank goodness no one drove by.

Tractors:
Oh! A Dam Tractor

The first tractors were built around 1850 and were operated by steam; they didn't become popular until the early 1900s. Wood, coal or straw was used for fuel to keep the water hot. We used coal because there wasn't much wood in our area. If the water tank ran dry while the fire was still burning it would explode. Many exploded because of flimsy or imperfect construction.

First tractor

Our first tractor was only used for grinding grain and filling the silo. It was not satisfactory in the field because it was so slow horses walked faster.

The first gasoline tractors were built in the early 1900's. They were started with a flywheel that was two-and-one-half feet in diameter fastened to the side of the tractor. It had places in which to put our fingers for a good grip so we could turn the wheel. After the tractor started it had a magneto acting as a battery to keep the tractor running. Later tractors were made with cranks. Two pins were welded to the crankshaft and the crank had two hooks that hooked onto these pins. Sometimes when trying to start the tractor it would kickback, therefore we only lifted up on the crank. If we went around and it kicked back when we were pushing down it would break our arm. Our next tractor was a John Deere with lug wheels. If for some

Lug wheel

reason the tractor couldn't pull the load in the field the lug wheels dug down and the tractor would be stuck. It was quiet a chore to dig it out. We used it some in the fields but needed the horses in order to get the entire farm work—planting, cultivating and harvesting—done on schedule.

Next we purchased a larger tractor called a McCormick Deering. All the farm work was done with this tractor except at silo filling time and for the lighter work.

Andy was in the field for the day so he took extra gasoline, drinking water and a grease gun. His things were one block from US Highway 24. While he was at the other end of the field he saw someone by his things and when he got back the people had poured the gas into their vehicle. For some reason on that particular day I took lunch to him. I had to go back home and get him some more gas for the rest of the day.

I was tall enough to reach the pedals at the age of thirteen so I became a tractor driver. After all my siblings left home I was put in the field pulling the one-way. Sometimes when I made the corner I didn't have the strength to straighten the wheels so I put my foot on the steering wheel and pushed with all my strength. By the time I got the tractor headed in the correct direction I had made a complete circle at the corner of the field. I was Andy's free "hired" help.

I had been out in the field a lot and I was tired of the noise. Andy always took the muffler off saying the tractor had more power and since the flywheel was used to start this tractor, and I didn't have the power to turn the flywheel I never shut the tractor off. There were no shade trees to rest under while eating. The only shade was the tractor wheel so I had to listen to that awful sound. My ears hurt after several days so one day I shut the tractor off at 4:00 pm instead of 5:30 or 6:00 as he expected. I walked a mile to his house since I had no car and when I got there I was scolded for leaving the field so early. As if that wasn't bad enough, Mother scolded me again when I got home. Even worse, after my siblings left home Andy ran the farm and I was treated as a man. One of Andy's brother- in-laws was on one side of the hayrack while I was on the other. I was expected to keep up with them by lifting the bean piles or shocks of grain on to the hayrack as fast as they did.

John had a dam built in a draw a quarter mile from his house. At that time the only large moving dirt equipment were "Caterpillar tractors" with a blade on the front that moved the dirt to one side or the other and lifted high enough not to push soil when not needed. The Soil Conversation Service staked out where Joe, the Caterpillar operator was to move the dirt from and where to put it. John's son, Billy went out and picked up all of these nice new stakes with which to play. When he brought them into the house his mother Ruth made him take them back out and put them where he found them. He didn't realize they were there for a purpose. Billy watched Joe build the dam. The next Christmas my sister Ann gave Billy a Caterpillar tractor for a gift. Upon opening the gift and seeing the tractor he said, "Oh a Dam Tractor." He didn't know to call it a Caterpillar.

Filling Silo: Making Corn Whiskey

Corn was easy to grow in the dry plains of Eastern Colorado. Thus we had used corn stalks to make ensilage to feed the animals in the winter.

In the early years a corn knife was used to cut the stalk. The blade of a corn knife was twenty-four inches long, six inches wide and one-inch thick with an eight-inch handle. The corn stalks were loaded on the hayrack and taken to the feed yard. The ear was broken from the stalk and the cornhusks were removed and used for bedding. We shelled the corn for the chickens, turkeys and ducks. The ear was tossed in the pigpen to let them remove their own corn. Every evening we gathered the cobs for kindling. One year we grew so much corn we sold some of the cobs to the school.

Silo

The silo was used to store the ensilage. It was fifteen feet in diameter and fifty feet high. There were "windows" three feet square every three feet. The first one from the bottom was four feet high. This enabled us to get in and out of the silo and to pitch the ensilage out. As we filled the silo we had a heavy piece of metal that covered the windows. Fastened in front of the windows was a chute. This was also made of heavy tin in a half-moon shape so when we threw the ensilage out it hit this metal and slid down.

After the silo was built an "ensilage cutter" was purchased to chop the corn stalk into one inch long pieces. The ensilage cutter was anchored by driving strong long rods into the ground. There were three sections of pipe eight inches in diameter and twenty feet long that car-

Ensilage Cutter

ried the ensilage into the silo. They were secured to the top with wire and on the bottom they were fastened to the cutter with bolts. On the top there was a half shaped pipe open on the bottom that guided the ensilage back into the silo. The bottom was open so if something happened in the silo the operators on the ground could see and stop cutting corn. There were pipes two feet long and eight inches in diameter that brought the ensilage down inside the silo allowing Dad to put it where it was needed. They were fixed so Dad could unfasten them as the silo got full.

There was one pulley on the tractor and another on the stationery machinery, thresher, ensilage cutter and grinder. The drive belt ran between the pulley on the machine and the one on the tractor that was the power making the machinery work. The drive belt used for the ensilage cutter and the threshing machine was a 200-foot endless belt eight inches wide. The grinder used a twenty-five-foot belt.

On the ensilage cutter the corn was dropped in a trough acting as a conveyor that had a chain on each side with slats going across that carried the corn to the knives. It was dropped with stalk end first so the leaves and ears didn't hinder the smooth running as they entered the cutter. There was a very heavy wheel holding the corn down just before it entered the knives. The axel of this wheel was long and went through slots in the sides of the cutter. This allowed the heavy wheel to move up and down as more corn entered. Someone had to guide the corn into the cutter. This was dangerous

Drive belt and hayrack

as hands were sometimes lost in this process. There was a lever near the cutting knives that we could lift up and stop the corn in the trough.[13]

As Dad walked around in the silo he also guided the ensilage to the right place keeping it level. The ensilage needed to be packed firmly to preserve it. Dad walked all day taking extra care to tramp ensilage well round the walls. Imagine walking all day lifting your feet high enough to step over the loose green cut corn. Any of the children big enough to climb into the silo helped Dad pack the ensilage as any and all weight was very helpful. He was the principal packer and was still doing so at the age of seventy-two. Dad stopped for lunch; otherwise he stayed in the silo all day.

The first step in filling the silo was to cut the corn from the field with a "corn cutter". We owned a one-row corn cutter and two two-row corn cutters.[14]

This process was time consuming and took a lot of manpower, as the corn cutting and silo filling had to be done quickly. If the corn was cut and left on the ground too long the sun dried it causing it to lose all nutritional value. The most nutritious ensilage had kernels on the cob but green enough to ferment and was slightly sour to the smell and warm to the touch. In the winter the moist ensilage froze along the walls of the silo and had to be pried away.

Once when John was in the silo he didn't pry the frozen ensilage from the walls. When Frank went up into the silo to pitch down the ensilage he found it frozen four feet high and twelve inches wide all along the sides. They made sure John was never in the silo alone again.

My sisters took the team with the empty hayrack wagons to the field and brought the full ones back. When I was old enough I helped with this job during harvest time. The outside horse knew to go far enough out so his teammate wouldn't hit anything on the other side. We had no problem after we learned to make wide turns so we didn't hit the corner post or bump into something with the wagon. If horses are in harness or have a saddle on their backs and something drastic happens they go to the barn.

Two row corn cutter

One of the drawbacks in filling the silo was the wind. Sometimes it blew so hard that the drive belt was thrown off the pulleys. My brothers devised a portable windbreak taking boards and standing them up to shelter the belt.

The knives in the ensilage cutter and the corn cutters had to be sharpened twice a day; at noon and either in the morning or at night to have them ready for the next morning. While this chore was being done at noon the horses had time to rest.

For horses pulling a piece of machinery during the heat of the day was as hard work for them as any physical exercise is for us.

One year Dad got anxious and had the corn cut when it was just a little too green so juice started running out of the windows of the

51

Wind break and first tractor (see tractor on page 45)

silo. My brothers put fifty-five gallon barrels under the windows to catch this juice. Naturally every one figured this had some food value so Dad gave it to the pigs. He did not understand why his pigs could hardly walk. He had given them corn whisky and they were drunk.

To make corn whisky I was told to stand a stone jug upright in the silo. The jug was covered with cut corn and as the silo was emptied and we got to the jug it would be full of corn whisky. People said, "This was the best corn whisky ever made." I didn't know about this when Dad filled all those silos because the cattle herd increased and more feed was needed, so we dug two trench silos close to the field. What fun we could have had at no cost with all this good booze but it all went "down the drain." Darnn!

One time when my cousin George was guiding the corn in the trough his glasses fell out of his shirt pocket into the trough and were headed for the knives. I saw them and jumped from the wagon and ran up to the lever lifting it up. I didn't know where neutral was so when I pushed up on the handle I shoved it into reverse and the corn started to back out. I didn't want a mess on the ground so I pulled back down on the handle and the corn with the glasses started to go back into the cutter so I lifted up on the handle again. After several attempts George came up and took the handle and put it in neutral asking, "What is the matter?"

I said, "Your glasses are in there." He found them and gave them to me to take to the house. Fortunately, I had seen the glasses. Since cows swallow their food and chew it later this would have been quite dangerous. Had they gone into the ensilage the cows could have become very ill or even died. If a cow eats a piece of wire or nail it goes through the walls of the stomach and causes the cow to die.

After the invention of an ensilage cutter that could be pulled by a tractor and driven with the power take off shaft the work became easier. (The power take off is a device on the tractor that runs the machinery it is pulling.) This ensilage cutter cut and chopped the corn, loaded it in a truck or wagon right in the field. Some farmers put the ensilage in a plastic tube called a sausage. These were quite expensive. Now many farmers dump the ensilage on the ground in long piles and do the packing with a tractor. When completed it looked like a loose haystack. What used to take twenty men can now be done with three or four. Now they even have self-propelled ensilage cutters. In some parts of the country hay is cut in this manner and it is called haylage. We used corn except during the dust bowl days when we used soap weeds.

Cutting Feed and Making Pretty Hay

Mower

All farm machinery used to cut feed from the stalk had a drive wheel. A "mower" is a piece of machinery we used to cut the grains, feeds, hay and weeds with a six foot long sickle. It was longer on other equipment.[15] After the hay was cut we used a "rake" to put the feed in a pile so we could load in onto the hayrack and take it to the feed-yard.[16] When the "hay baler" came out we raked the hay into a row called a "windrow" for the baler to pick feed up as it went down the field putting it into bales.

The next invention to put the hay in the windrow was the "side

Dump rake

delivery rake." This time we went around the field putting the feed in one long row. If the hay wasn't thick enough, we went down the field one-way and came back putting more hay in the windrow. This way the baler didn't waste time trying to get enough to make a bale. Grain was never baled for feed because if too much grain was in a bale the livestock became ill.

Then manufactures made the "swather." It cut the hay or feed and put it in a row to be baled. Later came the "self propelled swather" meaning a tractor was no longer needed. One thing that couldn't be done was cut and bale the hay at the same time. Hay must dry for several days before it can be baled. We hoped it didn't rain after it was cut because the hay would turn brown and lose its food value. If we baled the hay too soon it molded in the bales. Cows do not like moldy hay and will only eat enough to stay alive. Horses get deathly ill on moldy hay and without medical help will die. We liked to bail straw as soon as we could before it rained so it would be a nice yellow color and soft texture.

The "baler" was used for alfalfa, grass and straw. It worked very much like the binder except some used twine and others used wire.[17] The standard bales were fourteen inches wide by eighteen inches high by forty inches long. Now there are square bales that are four feet square and eight feet long. There are round bales of many sizes.

Harvesting Crops: Selling Grain by Instinct

Beans were first harvested by pulling the plants out of the ground by hand before they were mature to keep the beans in the pods. The smaller children got down and picked up each bean that fell out of the pods. When my folks threshed the beans by hand and screened the beans in the wind, what missed the container, we picked up by hand.

Our first "bean cutter" was a two-row horse drawn cutter with knives on a slant like those on the corn cutter. These knives ran one inch under the ground cutting off the roots. Most farmer's wives and girls "piled beans". This was to gather the beans after they were cut putting them into piles. The women in the towns "hired out" to the farmers. They put these cut beans on piles two rows together across the field like they did the corn for ensilage or the bundles. Two piles from each side of the hayrack could be loaded at one time. The beans were taken to the feed yard and stacked waiting for the threshing machine. As machinery improved more land was farmed. The fields were too far from the farm buildings for the children to go but they still picked up the beans in the farmyard that came out of the hull after the stacks were threshed. The beans in the field were left on the ground.

Bean piler

The next bean cutter we had was a "bean piler." As it cut the beans they were dropped on a canvas with wooden slats fastened to it. The beans were elevated four feet high and dropped into a bucket device made of heavy screen. Again the operator dropped the beans in piles of rows across the field. Even with this newer piece of equipment the women went down the field making sure the beans were in nice piles and picked up any that were lost.

Header

At first the grain was cut with a "scythe." When it was almost ripe it was tied into bundles twelve inches in diameter, with straw as there was no twine, then placed into shocks waiting to ripen. My folk's first large piece of machinery was a "header" pulled by six horses. The header cut the grain ahead of the horses and had a cutting blade like the mowing machine but much larger. The grain was dropped on a canvas with wooden slats taking the cut grain to another canvas elevating it to the "header barge." A header barge is a hayrack with laths on two sides and wire all the way around. One side was low for

Header Barge

the header to drop the grain while the other side was higher to keep the grain from going over. This way larger loads could be taken to the feed yard waiting for the thrashing machine. As new machinery came into existence farming became easier. My folks purchased most of it. After the header came the "binder" that cut and bound the grain at the same time.

Binder

Next came the "combine" that did the work the header and threshing machine used to do and was run by the power take-off shaft. They are self-propelled cutting the grain, threshing it and putting it in a bin. When we got to the end of the field we emptied the grain into a truck. We took the wheat to the grain elevator and sold it or paid a storage fee waiting for a higher price or we took it home. Most farmers erected grain bins on their property. Grains like oats, barley and rye were fed to the livestock.

There was a section of land one mile from the house that the folks purchased because as we kept the heifers we needed more feed. In the center of this field was a low spot with no drainage. After a hard rain it looked like a shallow lake that we called a lagoon. Crops planted in this area could not survive. Two to four weeks after a rain the land was dry again. My brothers dug a ditch and drained it into the adjacent pasture that was lower. The terrain was level enough not to cause a river to form and as a result this field produced great crops.

One year in the lagoon we grew a lot of cane that was a millet type of grain. The seed is dark, almost black. The cane was cut with a binder and placed into shocks.

When it came time to harvest the cane my brothers who were always inventing something devised a knife (similar to a paper cutter) on a wagon box. As the cane was gathered my brothers lifted the bundle up to the wagon box. One of them was in the box chopping the heads off the grain. The remaining bundle was tossed onto the hayrack. The heads were threshed and the rest fed to the cattle during the winter. It seemed to me we had a granary full of cane seed. The next spring my folks sold the cane seed to other farmers.

We used a scale to weigh the seed because we sold it by the pound. We had a hanging scale that was four feet long. Three feet had slots cut into it to hang the "pairs" with numbers to tell us how much the grain weighed. The scale used two pairs, the small one was

Scale and pairs (close-up)

for weights less than one hundred pounds, and the large one was used for up to 350 pounds. One side had numbers for the small pair and the other side had numbers for the large pair, telling us how

Scale and pairs

much something weighed. There were two little knobs welded on each side of the scale one inch apart. The one welded on the long end had a hook to hang it up across the doors or the rafters. The other one was on the short end with a hook to hang the object to be weighed. We had to watch because when weight was put on the scale the long bar went up and the short end came down. We reached up and pulled down on the long end, hung the pair in the proper place balancing the bar telling what the item weighed. In order to keep this bar from going up and down real fast and hitting someone the pair had to be removed while holding onto the bar and letting it go back up slowly and then removing the weighted object carefully.

The men enjoyed guessing the weight of the sacks. They competed to see who could guess the closest weight. The farmers brought their own "gunny sacks" made from burlap material in many shapes and sizes from purchases they made at the feed store known as a "grain elevator". The reason for the different size sacks was because some products took more space than others to make one hundred pounds. These were the only kind of sacks we used. Today, I don't even know if there are burlap sacks.

One day a farmer and Dad were using their skills in guessing the weight of the sacks. We sold so much seed Dad could guess them on the dot or within two pounds but the farmers were always off by quite a large amount. In the process of weighing those sacks one farmer wasn't careful when using the scale and it hit him on the head. He paid for his seed. Several days later he came back for more seed. Again he and Dad guessed the weight of the sacks. The farmer picked up the sacks and threw them in his vehicle. Dad said, "Aren't you even going to weigh those sacks?"

"You guessed them so accurately the other day it is not worth getting hit on the head with your scale for a lousy two pounds. Thanks, but no thanks. I'll take your word for what you said they weigh."

In those days no one sued for things like the scale hitting the farmer on his head when he purchased the cane seed. A man's word was as good or better than any contract today. If they said they would pay you after selling a cow or the next time they sold their cream, they did.

Another crop grown in the lagoon was a "bumper crop" of wheat. A bumper crop means great production. The wheat grew so tall it came up to my Dads' shoulder. The heads were so heavy and full of wheat that the stems were not strong enough to hold it up so it started to fall. Because it was still too green to cut with the combine we had to cut it with a binder and shock it. Our binder cut a swath eight feet wide but because the wheat was so thick and heavy we could only cut a foot or two at a time. The binder could not elevate the wheat up to where it was tied into bundles if we tried to cut the full swath.

The only way we could get it into shocks was for four or five people to work on one shock at a time. One person had to hold up the first group of bundles as the other people built the shock around them. When we were almost finished with the shock, the person holding it up backed out while the other people placed bundles where we were standing. Holding the shock was usually my job because I was not strong enough to lift the heavy bundles.

In another year in this same field we grew a lot of corn and had several men help to pick it from the fields. The corn had to be mature and picked in the winter months. A team of horses pulled the wagon box over the rows that had already been picked. This is one time a nosepiece was put over the horse's mouth when working, otherwise they ate the corn that was in the row next to them. The men preferred a team of mules because the mules didn't eat the corn. There is a saying, "Men and horses eat themselves sick but mules quit when they have enough!" This was true. If a mule got loose and into a grain bin it never got sick. A horse will die if not treated immediately and sometimes with treatment we still lost them. A mule is the offspring of a male donkey and a female horse and is usually sterile.

Picking corn was hard on the shirtsleeves. When we broke the ear the sleeves rubbed against the dry stalks wearing them out. Mom made a protective guard from worn out denim jeans and my brothers put them over their shirtsleeves.

Horses can have an innate sense. As we walked beside the team they automatically walked with us. When the team had gone far enough we hollered "WHOA" and they stopped. As we moved they started walking again and we never had to give the command "get up." When the wagon box got full it was taken to the feed yard.

On nice days in the spring we sat by the pile of corn and took the husks off. We had a band around our hands with a hook to catch the husks to loosen them away from the corn. We grabbed the ear of corn and pulled the husks away completely. The corn was placed in another pile waiting for the threshing machine.

After the corn threshing our next project was to sort the corn for seed. We used a "grader" to sort the round from the flat kernels. It was made of metal twelve inches in diameter and stood on legs high enough to put two five gallon buckets underneath to keep the kernels separate. The first half had round holes for the round kernels

Corn Grader or Sorter

to drop through and the last half had flat holes for the seed corn with a hole at the far end for the rest. There was a funnel on top at the front for us to pour a can of corn into the grader as we slowly turned the crank. If the grader was too full it didn't work correctly.

We saved what we needed for seed, sold some for seed, fed some to the livestock and sold the rest.

Courtship Ritual of Dunking

The next spring after corn picking, and the day after Easter two of the men who picked corn and two of their friends decided to give Helen and Mary a dunking. They believed that on the day after Easter the young ladies were to "cooperate and get dunked." The next day the girls were to go to the men's house and give them a dunking thereby starting a courtship. My sisters never wanted to date any of those men and didn't tolerate this stunt. Helen told me, "I was sitting at the table finishing my lunch and one of the men never said a word but took some water and walked to where I was sitting. He was dressed very nicely in a suit and he poured the water on me. I stood up and whatever I had left in my plate I dumped on him. I was very angry." He left and went to the barn.

Someone held the girls while the others tried to dump the water on them saying, "Just put your head above the slop bucket and we'll pour a small amount of water on you." One of the girls hit the dipper and water went everywhere. That started a water fight. Dad was sitting at the table and never got a drop on him. After the buckets were empty they moved to the porch where they continued with the water fight. We had washed clothes that day and the water they used was the water in which we had done the laundry.

The man in the suit was named George. I think he went looking for sympathy from my brothers because Frank came and witnessed the water fight. He saw his sisters being abused and grabbed two of the men around the necks holding them while one of my sisters poured water on the guys. George came back in looking for his buddies. He was ready to go home. What a surprise he received! He thought he had received his unwanted welcome the first time he was in the house only to find himself now on the concrete floor of the porch with his trousers being used as a mop for all the water. Unfortunately, he was still in them! I guess his friends felt that since he was not around to help them he did not deserve their help. Besides they were wet enough. That was the first and last time any one came to our house to give the girls a dunking. I'm sure word got around their neighborhood concerning what had happened.

Threshing Grain: Telling Stories

Threshing machine

Mom said, "The first threshing machine was turned by hand with a grinder type crank." Unfortunately I never found out from her how many men it took to turn the crank. It is no longer used today because combines do the job. Inside the threshing machine were screens that rubbed together and separated the grain from the straw. There was a wheel that blew the straw out of the thresher. Remember I described what happened in Europe when the farmer held the bucket of grain above his head and the breeze blew the straw away? This is the same principle. Grain being heavier falls down where an auger took the grain out to the side and dropped it into cups that elevated the grain up into a grain wagon. The screens had different settings for different grains.

Because the threshing machine was so expensive few farmers owned one. It was customary for a farmer to go from farm to farm and do the threshing for hire. When a threshing machine was in the vicinity all the neighbors gathered and helped each other. No one kept track of the hours spent working.

During harvest time whenever a farmer needed help all he had to do was ask and the other neighbors in the area pitched in and were available until the farm or household project was done. This was their way of survival. When help was needed not only men and women joined in the task of harvesting but also horses, hayracks and grain boxes were brought to accomplish these huge projects. The neighbor women helped cook the noon meal for all the threshing crew. There were usually fifteen or more men to feed. Everyone worked up a hearty appetite. There was always meat, potatoes, gravy, a vegetable or two of some kind and always dessert. Ah! What delicious meals they were. The house got so hot with the coal cook stove going all day. In addition to cooking the meals and heating water for the men to wash, we also heated water to wash the dishes after the meal. We called the noon meal "dinner" and the evening meal "supper." We never fed the harvesting crew supper. Often we had one of our foreign dishes at this time.

To earn extra money my brothers followed the threshing machine crew for several weeks until the boys were needed back home. Helen went to help the other housewives with the cooking. Desserts were usually made the afternoon before. Many days Helen spent all day at the neighbors helping with the preparation of the meals.

When beans were threshed some fell out into a pile by the threshing machine. By the end of the day there was a nice pile that contained rocks and hulls. Mom put these into sacks because they needed to be cleaned for market, as the price was lower if there were too many rocks. In the winter after supper she brought them in and put a pile on the table. We all sat round the table in the evenings cleaning the dirt out of the beans. Many winter nights were spent in this manner.

While we were cleaning beans one night after Halloween, Frank said, "Mr. Baker was tired of always having to put his outhouse back upright after the pranksters tipped it over, so he decided he wouldn't let them tip his outhouse over this year. He took his shotgun and sat in his outhouse with the intention of scaring them away. The pranksters didn't want to be seen from inside the house so they always came in from the back and tipped it over onto the front. Those pranksters quietly tipped Mr. Baker's outhouse towards the house landing it on the door trapping Mr. Baker inside." Frank continued with his story, "When he didn't come back into the house by the time Mrs. Baker was ready for bed she became anxious and went to see where her husband was. Finding him trapped in the outhouse she went to seek help. As I was driving down the street she stopped me and told me what happened. She asked if I could help her release Mr. Baker. I found some other people to help and we got him out." Mr. Baker never caught the pranksters.

Mother told us of the time she went to the grocery store and not knowing how to speak English she said, "Me vont dot."

The clerk said, "What?"

Mom said, "Vater go trou, mocorony stop."

The clerk left and returned with a colander and asked, "Is this what you want?' That was exactly what she wanted.

One night Mary wanted something from the bedroom and she asked me to get it for her. The coal-oil lamp was lit in the kitchen but it never gave off much light and because it was so dark I couldn't see that the door to the bedroom was closed. I was very young and afraid of the dark. I tried to be brave and went into the living room but wouldn't go any further. I stood in the living room facing the bedroom. My siblings kept saying, "Go on, nothing will hurt you!" I still stood back. Finally they said, "Make a run for it!" I finally did only to bump into the closed door. I didn't seriously injury myself from the impact, as I don't remember any pain.

On another occasion, when we were cleaning the beans, Mary told us of her experience that day at school. She said she needed a protractor and not wanting to attract the attention of the whole room she whispered to the boy sitting in front of her, "Do you have a protractor?"

Billy answered, "No, but I have a John Deere Tractor." Those nights spent cleaning the beans were often filled with laughter and fun.

Paul left home when he was young. I couldn't remember him and when he came home I told him this was not his home and Mom was not his mother. He had several stories to tell of his time out in the world. He was picking corn for a farmer in Nebraska when his boss said, "I bet you the price of a day's wages that you can't fill this wagon box full of corn by noon."

Paul had picked corn for a number of years and knew he could do it so he said, "I bet I can. You're on." Paul started down the field and not hearing the corn hit the bottom of the wagon box stopped and told us, "I looked back and all the ears of corn that I picked were on the ground where the wagon box should have caught the corn. The boss had removed the bottom of the wagon box."

Another story Paul told was even too much for me. Paul said, "This farmer was in the field when he saw a dark cloud in the sky. Knowing it was a tornado he watched it for a while and then deciding it was not coming his way went on about his work. The tornado changed its course and came by where the farmer was working picked him up, took him to the tornado shelter, opened the door, threw the farmer in and shut the door." I think Paul was "pulling my leg" but I guess it was a way of entertaining us while we were cleaning those beans. I do know tornadoes can do strange and weird things.

Still another one of Paul's stories went as follows, "At one time a railroad section boss named Jones owned a farm right by the tracks. His job was to hire men to help keep the railroad in good running order for the heavy freight trains and the fast passenger trains. This particular year Mr. Jones had pinto beans planted in the fields by the tracks. He stopped beside his field with the handcar and

Railroad hand car

had all of the employees help pile beans instead of working on the railroad. Unfortunately for him his boss came by at that time. Mr. Jones was no longer section boss!"

Handcars were used on the railroad to carry the spikes, railroad ties and anything else needed to repair the railroad. If more railroad ties were needed than would fit on the first car another car was fastened behind. Two people pumping a handle up and down like a teeter-totter operated the first handcar. When gas motors became popular the handcar was motorized. Now a pickup is used that has wheels like the handcar. When they get off the tracks they lift the metal wheels up and drive on the highways.

The Best Recipes

Dad and Mom came from a poor country and here are a few of our favorite recipes.

Haluski—Natural Dish of Slovakia

Sometimes haluski were made in beef soup. Haluski were made using soft noodle dough by mixing together one-cup flour, one large egg, one-half cup of water and a pinch of salt. Mom brought the water to a slow boiling point. Using an old spoon she cut off pieces of dough the size of small walnuts and dropped them into the boiling water. She dipped the spoon in the hot water after cutting every two or three haluski to keep them from sticking to the spoon. If the water wasn't boiling hard enough the haluski sank to the bottom and stuck. If it was boiling too fast the first ones were done and the last ones were still raw. While she was cutting the raw ones the pot had to be stirred to keep them from sticking together even when the water was at the right temperature.

Making haluski took less time than noodles so we had them more often. Mom sometimes put them in our chicken soup when time was limited. The holuski had to boil longer than noodles because they were thicker. After they were done Mom drained the water off and rinsed them in cold water or they tasted like flour. She quickly drained the cold water from the haluski then put them into the soup. Meals consisted of soups, a lot of pastas, noodles and breads. Desserts were krepya a doughnut made from some of the bread dough cut into squares fried in hot lard. Kolachi is a baked sweet bread and can be purchased in the United States, but the origin lies in the Slovak area of Europe.

Haluski and Caposta

Caposta means cabbage. Mom finely diced three cups cabbage using one sixteenth teaspoon salt and sautéed it slowly in a small amount of lard, just enough to keep it from scorching. While the cabbage was cooking she used one-cup flour and made haluski using the above recipe. After rinsing them quickly in cold water she poured fried butter over them using two walnut sized pieces of butter, and then added the cooked cabbage. To make fried butter she put it in a skillet and fried it until brown. (Today's' butter does not brown like the butter we used to make on the farm). Yum! This was one of our favorites. Since we were Catholic and didn't eat meat on Friday this was a very good and inexpensive meal for us.

Perohi

"Perohi" was another of our favorites. Mom did not make them very often because it took a long time. We had these only once or twice a year. Using the recipe from holuski she made noodles putting in a variety of different fillings. After the noodle dough was rolled out and cut into four-inch squares we put in a spoon full of the filling. Then we took one corner across making a triangle. We pinched the dough together firmly making sure it sealed in the filling. We boiled them until the noodle dough was cooked. We rinsed them quickly in cold water to remove the flour then poured hot fried butter over them and sprinkled with sugar. We kept the perohi with the different fillings separate.

One of the fillings was cottage cheese. It was the cheese we made from our milk and was dry. Into two cups cheese Mom mixed a raw egg and a little salt and sugar to taste. Another filling was cooked prunes. We really liked the poppy seed ones. She ground the poppy seed added one egg and enough sugar to taste depending on the bitterness of the poppy seed, usually one cup poppy seed and three-fourths cup sugar. Then she mixed it with enough milk to make paste boiling it for several minutes until thick. It was cooled before putting it on the dough. She also used this same filling in bread dough for kolachi. There were two other dishes Mom made that did not take as long as perohi, called "The Lazy Man's Perohi." These were not as good as the original ones. Mom made noodles but cut them wider than she did for soup. After she cooked and rinsed them in cold water she poured fried butter over them. She sprinkled in a small amount of sugar then added cottage cheese. For another dish she sprinkled enough sugar to taste then added the ground poppy seed. She didn't use much sugar because it would be too sweet and make us sick. Further, sugar was considered quite a delicacy in those days and was used very sparingly.

One of the things mother made that I really liked was an egg noodle drop soup. She didn't make it very often because it used so many eggs. She beat two eggs and one-third cup flour (this varies depending the size of the egg used) in a separate bowl for every two cups of broth. She heated the soup to a medium boil and cut the dough like she did for haluski and caposta but she put this dough right into the soup.

Many a winter night Mom made beans for our supper, especially if she happened to make bread that day. Otherwise she made biscuits using the cracklings of the rendered lard and substituted it for her shortening. That was yummy, too!

Sometimes I wonder if we were healthier because we ate a lot of things like beans. Mom always put a few lentils in our vegetable soup, using rice in her beef soup and barley in her pork soup.

Deaths Hit our Family Hard

There was a flu epidemic in 1911 and in 1918 but we were fortunate because we were not affected. When the polio epidemic (Poliomyelitis, also known as Infantile Paralysis) plagued the area in 1946 we were also fortunate. No one in our family contacted this crippling disease. The young infants were affected by it in the beginning. Besides taking many lives and leaving children and adults crippled, this disease left scars in the hearts of people in the community. Adults also contacted this disease, and then in older life they developed complications as a result. The flu epidemic in 1920 and 1922 affected us.

In 1920 the flu epidemic struck taking George who was two years old. The after effect of the flu was pneumonia and that is what caused his death. Mike was a baby at this time but he didn't get the flu.

In 1922 tragedy struck the family again this time taking Mike during another flu epidemic. Steve was quite ill when Mom was at the doctor's office with Mike. The doctor said, "Mrs. Kochis, you have a very sick baby."

Mother replied, "He's just fussy."

"No, ma'am, he has the flu." The doctor took care of Steve saving his life. He now has a permanent scar on one of his lungs and when he gets a TB test it is always positive but in further checking it is negative. My folks were very heartbroken by the death of their two boys.

Then to lose Joe only three years later, what a tragedy! In 1925 Joe was accidentally shot. Dad's nephew from Pennsylvania was visiting us for the summer. He went rabbit hunting with my brothers on the Big Sandy River. On the way home they did some target practicing. After several shots Joe said, "I'll see if you hit the target," and ran to the point where my brothers and cousin were aiming. Our cousin had possession of the gun at this time when it accidentally went off hitting Joe. Joe's last words were, "You shot me."

When my brothers carried Joe home Dad said, "I told you boys not to go but you wouldn't listen." Dad took it very hard. He could never write to his sister telling her what happened because every time he tried to write he cried so hard he was never able to finish the letter.

Several years later John went on a "bumming" trip. He worked when he needed money for food and other essentials. He walked or rode a freight train; hitch hiked or traveled any way he could to get around without spending his hard-earned money. He traveled over most of the United States. During that time he stopped at Dad's sister and told them about the accident and Joe. This was my Aunt's first knowledge of the fatality. She had wondered why Dad no longer wrote to her. When she heard that Joe was killed and her son had possession of the weapon she thought Dad was angry with her.

Dad and Aunt Joanna went many years without corresponding. In the mid 1940's when her husband passed away she notified us. Mom, Dad and Kate attended the funeral. After all those years Dad and Aunt Joanna became reacquainted again. She came to Colorado several times to see Mom and Dad before she passed away.

The Oldest Girl Leaves Home
at Age Twelve

Kate, the oldest girl was twelve when she left home, nine years before I was born. She and a cousin and a friend went to Colorado Springs with the intention of joining the convent. The friend became a nun but our cousin was working in the hospital cleaning bedpans so she went back home. Kate said, "I left home right after WW I in 1917. I worked in Saint Francis Hospital in Colorado Springs for $8.00 a month including board and room. I worked in the kitchen all day seven days a week preparing all three meals and doing the dishes. We never had any days off. Coming from the farm I was used to working every day. I shortly found a better paying job in Woodmen, Colorado, at the TB Rehabilitation Center ironing clothes for $14.00 a month board and room. In the mid 1930's I worked in a Laundromat closer to downtown Colorado Springs pressing clothes for eighty cents an hour."

One weekend Kate brought her boyfriend Bob, home with her. He was trying to tell my brothers how to do something. It didn't work and my brothers got disgusted and decided they would teach him a lesson. Fortunately, that night there was no moon so Bob couldn't see what the boys were doing. They put some rocks in their pockets. They drove the car two miles from home and took Bob into the middle of the pasture to go snipe hunting, telling him how delicious they tasted. Bob was to hold the sack for the snipes. Bob said, "What do snipes look like?" The boys said, "Just hold the sack and we will bring them to you."

The boys left Bob in the middle of the pasture while they all went in different directions. When they got far enough away so he couldn't see they returned and brought the rocks and put them in the sack. They told Bob not to rest the sack on the ground and hold it tight or the snipes would get out. They really stressed he had to hold the sack off the ground and said they were going back for more snipes. Leaving him they went to the car.

They had parked on a hill so they gave the car a push to get it started so Bob didn't hear them leave. He stood out in the pasture until his arms hurt from holding the rocks. It was after midnight

74

before it dawned on him the boys took him for a sucker. Bob had to walk home. He was furious but he learned not to try and tell my brothers how to do something he knew nothing about. Shortly after that Bob and Kate quit dating.

We made ice cream every time Kate brought friends from Colorado Springs. We had our own ice when it was cold enough. Sometimes it wasn't cold enough to freeze ice in the stock tank but all the snow hadn't melted in the little creek a quarter mile west of the house so we used snow. Otherwise we went to Limon for ice. We used half milk, half cream, eggs, sugar and vanilla to make ice cream. If we filled the

"ice cream freezer" too full the cream ran over. Ice and salt were added alternately as someone turned the crank. We made sure the drain hole was open to drain the salty water or it got into the ice cream. If we put in too much salt the ice cream froze to the sides faster than the paddles could scrape it away. Once it froze so hard to the sides the center never got cold enough so it never froze to make ice cream. When we used snow a vacuum

Ice cream freezer

formed two inches from the bottom of the bucket because snow is not solid. If this happened the ice cream never froze so we took a stick and kept poking it through the snow making sure that a vacuum didn't form. Homemade ice cream tastes much better than what is purchased at the store like other homemade and homegrown foods.

Later Kate met Ted and they dated several years before they married. He seemed to have trouble holding down a job so he stayed with us for eight months. Food was not plentiful during the depression so we ate what was available and made do with what we had. One thing we had was Jack Rabbits. There was a saying; "It is safe to eat wild rabbits in a month that had the letter "R" in it, otherwise leave them alone." They can weigh five pounds after dressing.

Ted made the comment, "All winter we ate jackrabbit, potatoes and beans. When we got tired of that we ate beans, potatoes and jackrabbit and when we got tired of that we ate potatoes, jackrabbit and beans." I thought he should have been thankful to have a place to stay and something to eat. Ted was with us on his birthday and said he wanted us to make him a pie instead of a cake.

We asked him, "What kind of pie do you want?"

"I only like three different flavors!"

We wanted him to like the pie so we asked," What were they?"

He answered, "Hot, cold and warm." He was strange at times.

Then one year at Easter when Ted was 45 he was showing off to see how many eggs he could eat. He ate thirty or more hard-boiled eggs. During the night he became so ill Kate had to take him to the ER. Guess what? One of the foods the doctor put him on was soft-boiled-eggs. He learned his lesson.

One day during the time Ted stayed with us he and sister Helen were going to Denver in Ted's car. The doors had a tendency to come open. Helen had some white plates on her lap and her white purse on top of the plates. On the way to Denver the door came open and Helen's purse fell out. She didn't know it until she arrived in Denver. Travelers on their way to Denver found Helen's purse. They passed Ted on their way and when they went into the hotel restaurant they told the waitress, "We are traveling through Colorado and found this purse. What shall we do with it?" Upon opening the purse they found it belonged to Helen. Everyone was very surprised. The waitress was none other than my sister Ann. We all laughed that Ann knew Helen was on her way to Denver and she always said, "Helen's purse arrived in Denver before she did."

School: Games: Hot Lunches: Parties

The summer my folks built the house the school district built a one-room school called "Twin Meadows for grades one through eight a quarter mile north of the home place." There was a barn in

School House

the back for horses that some students rode to school. The outhouses were also built behind the schoolhouse that was in the center of the plot. Our playground was in front of the school. At one time there were thirty-two children enrolled. That was a huge number for a one-room school and one teacher.

All of my siblings and I attended this school. Mom said, "The boys would be at the barn doing chores when it was time for school. When the teacher rang the bell the boys dropped what they were doing and ran to school. The teacher continued ringing the bell until they arrived thus not counting them tardy." The girls took the boys' lunches when they went.

My older siblings had only one change of clothes. Mom washed and ironed their clothes at night while they slept so they could have clean clothing for school the next day. Our wardrobe consisted mostly of hand-me-downs and whatever Mom would sew for us. We went barefoot in the summer.

We wrote on blackboards in school using white chalk. There were two in the front of the room and two in the back. We used an eraser after finishing our lessons so the next class could do their lessons. At the end of the day two students took the erasers outside and pounded them on the cement foundation to remove the chalk. The teacher wiped the boards with a damp cloth twice a year otherwise they got so white from the chalk that we were unable to read what we had written. Later green boards were used with the white chalk.

There was very little paper so we did not have the opportunity to practice writing. The teacher taught us penmanship. The only thing we had to write on was a tablet that cost a dime, and was labeled "Big Chief" with a large number "100" on the front with 100 pages in it. The paper was so porous we only used pencils with which to write. If we used ink, the letters just blended together.

Our pencils were called penny pencils since they cost only a penny and had hard lead. They had a small eraser on the tip. Our first ink pen was the Quill pen, a feather we dipped in liquid ink. We would find a tail or wing feather and cut the tip off at an angle making a sharp point leaving the fan of the feather. It became a game to see who came to school with the nicest feather. We dipped the sharpened end of the feather in the ink, wrote several words and it was time to dip the feather in the ink again.

Fountain pens with metal tips became available. When we dipped it in the ink, it wrote a few more words than with the feather pens. The tip usually got bent and it had to be replaced. Then fountain pens had a rubber tube that we filled with ink. We could write all day without filling this pen if we were lucky and it didn't leak all over leaving an awful mess. Otherwise they were great. Ballpoint pens became popular after WW II.

A well was dug on the school grounds but the water was not good because it was never pumped and the well caved in. One teacher had a three-gallon container and brought water to school for us. When it was hot we often ran out of water so the teacher sent one of the other students and one of my siblings or me to our house for water. Other times we carried our own water always making sure we had brought enough to last on the hot days.

When the weather was too bad to have school we had makeup days. For every day that the school was closed on weekdays, we went to school on Saturdays. This allowed us to close for summer vacation at the scheduled time. I'm sure our parents were glad to get us out of their hair on those cold Saturdays. In the spring there was the garden to plant, baby chickens that needed attention, and the farming. By then it would be warm enough to play outside.

We also had fun during our school days at recesses that consisted of fifteen minutes twice a day at mid morning and mid afternoon. Lunches were usually thirty minutes and after we finished eating we ran out to play.

One of our games was "Hide and Seek." One person was "It" and they hid their eyes against the school which was the base counting to twenty-five, or if we wanted to teach the "It" person to count by fives they then counted to one hundred. While they were counting that gave the rest of us time to hide. When the person who was "It" saw you, the point of the game was to see if you could run and touch the base saying "Free" before the "It" person said, "one, two, three for (the persons they saw)." If they did it before we said free then we were caught. The person who was "It" went from one side of the schoolhouse to the other to see if they could catch one of us peeking to see if we could run in free. The secret was not to get caught. After everyone was caught the first person caught was "It" for the next game.

"Kick the Can" was similar except a can was placed ten feet from the schoolhouse that was the base. One of us kicked the can and while the person who was "It" went and got the can and put it back on base the rest of us went and hid. When the person that was "It" saw one of us they put their foot on the can and said, "One, two, three for (the person they saw)". Sometimes when the "It' person was counting for one of our classmates another one of us ran around the corner and kicked the can out from under the persons foot. When this happened we all ran and hid again. Instead of getting in free we kicked the can and all the students that were caught up until then got to go and hide again and the "It" person had to start all over catching people.

I think "Fox and Geese" was our favorite. When there was enough snow on the playground we made a big circle in it with four spokes. The center was home base and the person who was "It" touched anyone that was not on base then that person was "It." Even after the snow was gone we played in those tracks until they were no longer visible.

Another game was "Black Man." We drew lines for two bases across the schoolyard four feet away from the fence for one base and six feet away from the schoolhouse for the other. Again the person who was "It" stood in the center while the students ran across the schoolyard from base to base. Once we left the base we could not go back, we had to continue across. If the person who was "It" touched one of us, then we helped catch the rest of the students. The first one caught was the "It" man for the next game.

Then there was "Anti Over". We chose sides, one for each side of the schoolhouse. We tossed a rubber ball over the top of the school. If we didn't catch it we shouted anti over and threw the ball back. If someone caught it we ran around to the other side and tagged everyone we could with the ball. Then they were on our side. When we threw the ball we hollered "Anti-Over." Sometimes when we caught the ball we yelled "Anti-Over," then ran around and caught people because they were looking up for the ball to come back over the schoolhouse.

We never had enough students to have two teams for softball so we played "Workup Soft Ball." When the batter got put "Out" they played in the outfield. The next person that was "Out" went to play in the outfield and the previous person moved to third base. As each person was put "Out" everyone advanced around the bases until we got to bat. If we were good at batting and luck was with us, we could be at bat for a long time; otherwise it was our turn to be in the outfield.

"Red light" was tricky. The "It" person hid their eyes and while they said, "One, two, three, Red Light" we moved down to the other end of the playground as fast as we could before they turned round. If we were still moving and they saw us, we had to come back to where we were before they had started counting.

"May I," was educational. The person who was "It' told us to do various things. One was take baby steps, take chickens steps, take giant steps or do a monkey turn. When the "It" person told us to do one of these things and if we did them without saying "May I" we had to go back to where we were and miss our turn. It got boring after we remembered to say, "May I."

On cold days we played "Simon Says." That game was tricky. The person who was "It" would say "Simon Says Thumbs Up" and moved their thumbs to that position then everyone put their thumbs up. The trick was to say "Simon Says" thumbs up or down or in or out with speed and then not say "Simon Says," just say up, down, in or out and see how many people follow what they did. If we changed positions when the "It" person did without the command then we were out of the game. The last one that didn't change positions without the command "Simon Says" won and got to be the "Simon Says."

"Hide The Thimble" or "I Spy" was another indoor game but since we didn't have a thimble we used a small piece of chalk. We went out into the cloakroom while the person that was "It" hid the chalk in plain sight. Sometimes we ran out of places so if it was hidden to where it could only be seen from a certain place they had to tell us. When we found the chalk we said "I spy" and when the rest of the students saw what way we were looking they found it easily. Then we got smart and when we saw the chalk we turned around and said "I Spy" and everyone looked in the direction we were facing. Again the first person spying the chalk got to hide it for the next game. If someone had a hard time finding it and they were across the room we said, "You are cold." When they got closer we said, "You are warmer," and if they were right by it we said, "You are burning up."

Eventually the school got two swings and a monkey bar for us to play on during recess.

One year we each took a raw potato to school in the winter and the teacher put them in the ash box of the heating stove. As the hot ashes dropped on the potatoes this cooked them and by noon we had a hot baked potato with our lunch. One day a student brought such a large potato to school that it didn't have time to bake before lunch so he didn't get to eat his potato.

When the weather got cold one of our teachers, Mrs. Groff, had us bring something we could heat on the stove to share with the other children. She felt the attendance was better with something hot to eat every day in the cold months. She always brought something on Mondays, which she prepared over the weekend. Our favorites were beans that she made with a lot of tomatoes but she never gave us her recipe. Each family was assigned a day to bring the surprise hot food to go with our sandwiches. She put the kettle on the potbellied coal stove to heat. We each brought a cup and spoon of our own. The cup could be used to drink from or we used it to eat our soup or beans.

The Christmas program was the highlight of the year. The students acted out plays portraying the Christmas story or other plays memorizing their speeches. Even the littlest ones had their parts in these plays. How embarrassing when someone behind the curtain had to give you a cue. We sang the beloved Christmas carols, many times getting the audience to join in on the last chorus.

There was a tree to decorate. My older siblings made paper chains and ornaments. We had shinny tinsel and the treasured ornaments from past years. Since there was no electricity, on the tips of the branches were small candles in clip-on metal holders that were lit but soon extinguished because of fire danger. We drew names and gave that person a gift. We did our best not to let the person know whose name we drew but tried to find out what they would like for a gift. Then Lo and Behold! Here came Santa from outside in his bright red suite ringing the school bell. Eyes sparkled and hearts rejoiced as Santa handed out the gifts. At last it was over and the gifts were admired. It was so much fun!

We didn't have money for valentines. A week before Valentine's Day and after the chores were done we got out the seed catalog and with luck we may have wallpaper samples or white wrapping paper. The teacher gave us red construction paper to cut out hearts for our valentines. We made sure we cut a heart for each student and the teacher. Using the seed catalog with their pretty flowers, crayons, bits of ribbon and lace, we made glue with water and flour, gluing the red hearts, ribbon or lace to a piece of paper we thought looked best. What fun we had as we each tried to outdo the other making the prettiest valentine. We wrote different poems on the inside and put the name of the intended person on the front, and whom it was from on the back. The teacher decorated a box and put a slot on the top for us to put in our valentines. We hurried through afternoon classes so we could have a party. We played games and one I remember was a contest to see who could draw the best heart on the blackboard blind-folded. For the best heart the teacher gave a cute cupid valentine as the prize. Then it was time to pass out all the Valentines from the box. Someone was selected to hand out the valentines as the teacher read the names. Years later, we bought them two for a penny but that was not as much fun.

I thought it was a lot of fun to decorate eggs for Easter. We decorated the eggs on Thursday evening before Easter because we needed to have some for our school party on Friday. Most Easter mornings dawned nice and clear. Some days it would be cold enough to need a coat. Dad always hid the eggs. As soon as we woke up we grabbed a bucket and ran out to look for Easter Eggs. Our yard was large so it took some time to find the eggs. Before commercial Easter egg dye, we used beet juice to make pink eggs, boiled onion skins for beige or light brown, orange peal or ocher (one could use any of the various clays containing iron oxide, and varying in color from pale yellow to brownish-red, much used as pigments in paints) to make yellow and orange.

Mom always put salt in the water before boiling eggs to keep them from cracking. They were also easier to peel. Adding vinegar keeps the yolks from running all over should one break. Mom brought the eggs to a boil then removed them from the fire and let them stand in the hot water for eighteen minutes. Sometimes we had some hard-boiled eggs on the counter. If one of my mischievous siblings found one in a feed stack they brought it to the house putting it on the counter with the others. To tell the difference without breaking them, give it a spin and if they twirl around they are cooked. If they don't spin then they are raw. Except for Easter Mom tapped each egg with a spoon while running cold water over them to break the shell. This let them peel a lot easier. An easier way to peel eggs is to place them in ice water with a couple tablespoons of soda. After a minute or two tap the small end on the counter and remove a small amount of shell. Then tap the large end and remove a larger amount of shell. Put the small end to your mouth and blow. Don't forget to catch the egg as it will pop right out of the shell.

Literaries were good family entertainments at schools any time of the year. Schools got together, taking turns sponsoring them. The hosting school put on a play and anyone in the community with any kind of talent participated. There were singing, readings, playing musical instruments, recitations, spelldowns or ciphering-matches. Spelldowns were a spelling contest and ciphering-matches were a math contest. The pie socials and box suppers were part of the fun on those evenings and were good fundraisers.

Box suppers were held early in the evening because they were actually the supper meal. Pie suppers were held after a school play or some other event later in the evenings. We decorated a box large enough to hold the pie if it was a pie supper or one large enough to hold sandwiches, oranges, apples, cookies, or maybe some canned fruit. They were auctioned off to the highest bidder and the prettiest ones usually brought the highest prices. These were really fun because no one was to know on whose box they were bidding. Sometimes a girl told her boyfriend what her box looked like. Sometimes the boy's father or some older men caught on to who was bidding or they even bought the box because the boy didn't have enough money. If it were the boy's dad he'd be nice and let the boy and girl eat together. Sometimes if it was one of the older men they got ornery and outbid the boyfriend and actually ate with the young girl. How shy and embarrassing for the young girl. These probably started from the time the schools first needed money. We had paper plates by the time I was old enough on which to put the rest of the pie and let the bidder take it home. One time sister Ann made an extra pie but didn't put her name on it so when the boy bought it they didn't know what to do so he had his friends join him. They declared the bean and potato pie was delicious.

Frank and Helen registered for high school in 1929. They stayed home to help do the fall work bringing in the feed and canning the garden vegetables. When they finally went back to school the teacher said, "You have missed so much school and are so far behind it is impossible for you to catch up with the rest of the class." They never did get to go to high school.

Steve missed a lot of school because he was a strong boy and my folks had him stay home and help with the work. His grades were not the best so the teacher suggested he repeat the 8th grade. He stayed out of school one year and waited for Mary to graduate from the 8th grade. Steve and Mary started high school in 1937. When they went on their senior trip in early spring of 1941 they went to states south and east of Colorado. Somewhere in their travels they came to where there were fresh strawberries. Remember there was no refrigeration in those days, so you can imagine the excitement of fresh berries. Someone suggested strawberry short cake, only low and behold no eggbeater with which to make whipped cream for strawberry shortcake. My siblings said, "Buy the cream and we will make whipped cream. We don't need a beater."

The class asked, "How are you going to accomplish this task without a beater?"

Steve and Mary said, "Get the cream and we'll show you!" They had an empty jar from food. Putting the cream in the jar and shaking it like we made butter they made whipped cream. The class was amazed at this way of making whipped cream without an eggbeater and learned there is more than one way to do things.

I was the youngest child of the Kochis family and after I graduated from the 8th grade the school closed. Later, the school district took sealed bids for the schoolhouse. Andy put in a bid for $300 but decided if Dad put in a bid for more money he would get it free by having Dad pay the higher price. Therefore Andy had me put in a bid for Dad in the amount of $305. Since Dad's bid was higher the school district took it having Dad pay for the schoolhouse for Andy. He dug a basement and put the schoolhouse over it and used it for storage.

School children either walked or rode a horse to school. Teachers lived with families that were close to schools. The teachers of Twin Meadows School put up a tent in our back yard and lived there during the week going home for the weekend. One winter it was so cold that my folks let the teacher move into our unfinished back porch, because it was warmer than her tent. This was common until the mid 1930's, when cars became more popular. My teachers were all female until high school. In the early years a married female could not teach school.

Our First Cars

The first cars traveled twenty or twenty-five miles per hour. The cars that had the gas tanks under the front seat or in front of the dash had no fuel pumps like the Model T or the Model A. Gravity fed the gas to the motors. When the gas tanks that were under the seats weren't full the car couldn't get gas to go up steep hills so the passengers got out and pushed it. If there were no passengers they turned the car around and backed it up the hill. When a car broke down it could often be fixed using a screwdriver, a pair of pliers and a piece of bailing wire.

St. Agnes Catholic Church

When it was cold during the winter, the radiators froze while we were filling them. Many Sundays we didn't go to church because we couldn't get the car started. My brothers tried to start the car for thirty minutes or more before it was time to get ready for church by putting hot ashes under the motor hoping to warm up the oil. If the car started we bundled up and rode to church in a cold car. The first cars didn't have heaters. The church had a very high ceiling so that it was still cold even when the fire was built several hours before Mass started. Then we sat in a cold church for an hour and got back in a cold car to come home. By then we were so cold we felt like we were frozen. Many times someone went out and started the car during services or the radiator froze. Antifreeze was invented in 1926 but the Prestone leaked out of the smallest hole where water won't.

The first cars had four-inch wide tires and were made of hard rubber. The wheels were three feet in diameter with wooden spokes making the car high off the ground. This was so when it snowed the car could go through the snow. It did not take as much power.

If we were in mud the car was less apt to get stuck and we traveled on. There were no snowplows to clean the snow from the highways. The roads were dirt or gravel.

My folk's first car was a four-cylinder 1917 Rio. Their second car was a four-cylinder 1927 Chevrolet. The third car a six-cylinder 1936 Plymouth and it cost $850.00.

1917 Reo

Mom never learned to drive. Dad drove until one day he forgot to step on the brake and hit the barn. He got out from under the wheel and gave the job to my brothers.

To start the first cars we had to crank them. When the engine started the crank came loose and was put back into the car so it didn't get lost. The pins and crank had to be kept greased or the crank would stick and fly around once the motor started. These old cars also had to be choked especially when the weather and vehicle were cold. A rod was fastened to the choke in the engine to the front of the vehicle so the person who was cranking the car could choke it as needed. There was also a device on the dash or steering wheel so a person inside the car could choke it

1927 Chevrolet

1936 Plymouth

while the other one was cranking. We had to make sure the car was in neutral so when it started it would not run over us. One had to be careful as to how we held on to the crank while trying to start the car. Sometimes the engine would kickback causing it to reverse thus breaking an arm. Then other times when we tried to shut the engine off the motor ran in reverse if the car was not tuned correctly. When this happened the car rocked back and forth like a cradle because the engine was running backwards. To remedy this we turned the key back on and the motor ran again so we shut the engine off. If the engine ran backwards too long it could break the crankshaft and that was very expensive to replace.

In later years a starter was put inside the car and a special lever was on the dash to use as a choke. The starter was to the right of the gas pedal. Before starting the car we pumped the gas pedal a couple of times and then we pressed the gas pedal half way down with our heel and stepped on the starter with our toe. We had to be careful not to flood the motor with too much gas. It took a special knowledge to get everything correct. Later the starter was a button on the dash. All cars were made with stick shifts; in fact Model T Fords had three pedals. I never drove one so I have no idea why the third pedal was there. I have been told it is the gas pedal. We put the car in neutral and shut the key off when going downhill to save on gas. When the car was still moving we turned the key on and put the car in a gear to coincide with the speed while releasing the clutch and pushing on the gas throttle. This started the engine and we then shifted into higher gears as we picked up speed. We did not have power steering or power breaks so the engine didn't have to run in order for us to have control over those two devices. The windshield wipers worked on a vacuum. If we were pushing on the gas to go up a hill the wipers didn't move. We lifted our foot from the gas for them to work but it was next to impossible if traveling in the mountains. Driving those old cars wasn't very much fun.

We only had one car and everyone went together. If it was dancing on a Saturday night everyone went to the same dance. If it was the movies on a Sunday afternoon we all went to the same theater. There was a theater in Limon, Simla and Calhan. The theatres in Simla and Calhan closed in the mid 1940's.

Making Sheets: Making Soap

The settlers were resourceful and self-sufficient in all areas of their lives. When the sheets Mom bought became worn and torn in the middle Mom ripped them on down and hemmed the torn edges. She sewed the two sides together leaving the stronger part in the middle making them last longer. The next time they wore out she took the stronger corners and cut them into a piece of material twenty to thirty six inches square that we wrapped around our feet, smaller sizes for the little ones. These were our stockings. If we didn't wrap the material correctly it worked out of our shoes and made blisters. Sometimes the material made a blister anyway. Oh! Such pain!

Flour and sugar came in 100 pound white sacks and had their labels stamped on with a strong dye. After Mother emptied the flour and sugar in her special metal containers we washed these labels off using homemade lye soap and a "washboard." When Mom had extra flour or sugar sacks that we didn't need for tea towels she used five and made a top sheet.

We used a "washboard" to wash our clothes before washing machines were invented. A washboard is a heavy piece of galvanized steel framed with wood. The wooden side frame went down and had two legs on the bottom that held the washboard above the bot-

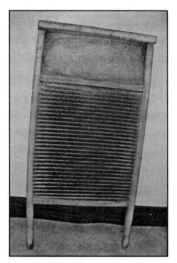

Washboard

tom of the washtub. There was a shelf fixed on the top for holding the bar of soap. The steel was corrugated and on the top of each corrugation were smaller corrugations that ran in the opposite directions of each other. This made it rough so the clothes could be washed clean with rubbing. It also wore sores on the knuckles by the time the weekly laundry was finished.

Mother made different kinds of soap; she liked the boiled soap best. To make it Mother used a big "cast iron" kettle. The kettle had three short legs long enough to keep the kettle from tipping over. Mom put bricks under the legs to raise it high enough to build a small fire under the kettle. She used her own recipe for the soap. I don't know the proportions but she put in some lye, water and the skins that were removed from the bacon before curing. She also used any leftover cracklings from the rendered lard and beef tallow. She started a fire in the morning and it slowly boiled all day. If the fire got too hot the contents started to run over and the fat from the mixture caught fire and went up the side of the kettle then all the fat in the soap would be ablaze. To stop the soap from running over we poured in a small amount of water but that only lengthened the time the soap had to cook. We had a long strong wooden paddle that reached to the bottom of the kettle that we used to stir the soap continually all day long. Mom stirred the soap over the lunch hour. When we were through eating we came out and relieved her so she could eat her lunch.

Another kind of soap was made in an enamel container. To make this she dissolved one can of lye in one quart of cold water and stirred until all the lye was dissolved. In a separate dish she put in one-teaspoon salt, two tablespoons sugar, three tablespoons borax, half a cup of water and then stirred thoroughly. She would continue to stir after adding each of the following ingredients, half-cup ammonia, the lye mixture and five pints of soft lard. The mixture is stirred until it thickens. Lastly she added one teaspoon of Anise oil for a pleasing fragrance.

We purchased fresh fruit in wooden crates and Mom lined them with an old piece of white material then poured in the homemade soap. As soon as the soap was firm we cut it into oblong pieces like the bars from the store. The soap had to age for several weeks. When it separated from the edge of the box and was hard it was mature enough to use. The lye in the soap made the clothes very clean. We hung the clothes on the line outside making the clothes smell fresh because the air was fresh and clean. The sheets smelled so fresh.

Heating Water:
Using a Wooden Washing Machine:
Using the "Sad" Iron

We heated our house with a heating stove and the cook stove. At first we had a "potbellied" stove in the living room. This stove was black and had no heat protector around the sides so the sides were as hot as the top and could be extremely dangerous. When the "circulating heating stove" was introduced the folks purchased one. This was much safer. It was like the potbellied stove but a square enamel protector around the outside made it real nice to sit with your back right up against. Our feet were still cold. If the fire in the stove was very hot the protector could get quite warm. There was an open reservoir in the back where we put water for moisture in the air. We had to push the stovepipe back into the chimney once a week or it would fall from the wall. One time we forgot. The stovepipe came out of the chimney and the house was getting full of smoke.

Potbellied stove

In the winter we put bricks and our flatirons to the back of the stove so they were warm. Before bedtime we wrapped them in newspaper and put them at the foot of our bed.

Our galvanized drinking water buckets were beside the cook stove and in the winter it got so cold the water froze. This happened even if Mom got up to rebuild the fire in the middle of the night. The water bucket had a dipper and when we wanted a drink we picked up the dipper and drank, then put it back into the bucket even if we never drank all the water. The dipper held a pint and was used for drinking and dipping hot water from the reservoir for washing our hands.

Cook stove

Copper boiler

Wringer

In the kitchen we had a "Home Comfort cook stove". I had never seen one like it at any one else's home. This one had a reservoir next to the firebox so the water got very hot. A reservoir is a tank that is attached to the stove so any time there was a fire we had warm water. On this stove the oven door was so strong we could stand on it if we needed to reach up high or we sat on it to heat our backs. Ah so warm! We usually kept the oven door open to heat the kitchen.

Washing clothes required muscle. We carried in water before the evening chores were started and filled the "copper boiler" on the back of the stove. It held fifteen gallons. The reservoir was also filled at this time and held the same amount. When Mom built the fire in the morning water started to heat so it was hot when we were ready to wash the clothes.

All the clothes were washed in the same water starting with the dress shirts then the whites followed with the colored clothes and finally the blue jeans. The dirtiest ones were put in last. Only one tub of water was used for rinsing. After the clothes were washed Mom put them through the "wringer" while we smaller children turned the crank. We were honored to turn the crank of the wringer giving us a feeling that we were a big help. This was a special piece of equipment that she used on laundry days and fastened to the tub. It had two rollers wringing out the water instead of having to twist the clothes. We had to fold the material over the buttons when putting the clothes through or the wringer ripped them off. The rollers were made of hard rubber and were replaced when they became worn.

Mother did keep her wringer after she got her washing machine. Mom's first washing machine was made of wood. She discarded it by the time I was five years old. I remember my older siblings played with it a few times. It was twenty-four inches wide and forty inches long standing on legs making the top waist high. The bot-

Wooden washing machine

tom was round. Inside the machine were two more half moon shaped boards to coincide with the rounded bottom. Attached to these boards were one-inch square boards as wide as the washing machine and fastened close together. They were on an angle so the corners of the boards rubbed against the clothes. It was operated on the side with a stick similar to a broom handle that was stuck into a piece of

Inside wooden washing machine

iron. By moving the stick back and forth gears moved the top section inside the machine like a swing thus agitating the clothes. A lid lifted up on the end to remove the clothes. I believe in using the machine for many years the edges of the little square boards wore away and left nothing to rub against the clothes to get them clean.

Her next washing machine was a gasoline-operated Maytag with a wringer attached. Maybe it was fine when it was new. I remember getting the tubs ready to wash the clothes and the machine full of very hot water but many times we couldn't get the motor started. The starter was a lever like the motorcycles have. We stomped on the lever trying to get the engine to run. We finally did the washing by hand. When my brothers came home for lunch they did something and stomped on the lever once and it started.

After rural electricity came to our place we put an electric motor on the washer so all we had to do was push the plug into the electric outlet.

Maytag washing machine

Even with the washing machine collars and cuffs on long sleeve shirts and blouses had to be scrubbed to get them clean. Mother always wore an apron and that got exceptionally dirty so it would be hand scrubbed before it went into the washing machine. We used the larger bar of soap in the washing machine so we could find it or too much soaked away by the time we emptied the water in mid afternoon.

We put "Bluing" in the rinse water to make the white clothes white and the colored clothes bright. A tablespoon in a tub of water did the job. It was very blue and if a person got it on a piece of clothing without water it would spot like ink.

After we got the clothes washed we had to hang them on the clothesline. Often it was ten o'clock in the morning before the first clothes were hung. We had to bring them in by four in the afternoon because it was time to start the farm chores. Sometimes the clothes were frozen stiff when we brought them in. I never felt that the clothes dried at all. I just hated to hang those clothes in the winter because my hands got so cold they hurt. It was wonderful in the summer time but what misery in the winter! We tried to pick a nice day for the washing but we didn't have the weather forecasts we do today.

The clothesline was as thick as a number four wire and before we hung the clothes it needed to be cleaned. We took a wet rag and wrapped it round the clothesline moving our hands back and forth while walking along the line changing the rag to a different position when it got dirty. The first clothespins were made from a round piece of wood with a slit cut in the center and were six inches long. The wood was very strong because we had to put the clothes on the line and then push the clothespin over the garment and the wire.

We had no way of knowing what the next day would be like for doing the laundry. We just hoped it would be a nice day since we hung the clothes outside. Finally John purchased a radio that was powered by a six-volt car battery. There was a lot of paraphernalia (tubes, fuses and other things I don't even know) that was needed to make the radio work. John built a bench to hold all the equipment. It had one set of headphones thus only one person could listen at a time. Since John bought it he wouldn't let anyone else listen but he went to bed leaving it on and fell asleep. The battery was dead the next morning. There was no easy way to charge the dead battery. Since there was no electricity we didn't have battery chargers. It would have to be put in a car to be charged and since we didn't drive our car very often we had little opportunity to charge a battery. When we finally went to town we took it to the garage.

Since all of our clothes were made of cotton and we starched them using a special starch made for clothes that was boiled. After it cooled we put in the collar and cuffs of shirts and blouses and wrung it out by hand. If the starch was too strong the clothing scratched our bodies. If they were not starched they had no body and if not ironed they looked worse than the wrinkled clothes that were so popular in the 1980's. Starching the work clothes helped to keep them cleaner. The blue jeans were starched as best we could with what was left. The starch stuck to the iron and the best way to get it clean was to iron a piece of waxed paper. The only wax paper we had was on a loaf of bread. Since we seldom bought bread we never had any wax paper because bread from the store was wrapped in cellophane. There was a piece of wax paper four inches wide wrapped around the center of the loaf of bread with the bakery label on it therefore we were always out of wax paper.

There were no ironing boards. We removed the oilcloth from the kitchen table and put down a blanket with a sheet on top and one

Sad iron

Flat iron

Gas iron

of those nice white flour or sugar sacks. The first ironing boards were made of wood and weren't adjustable. Later adjustable metal ironing boards took their place.

We dampened the clothes "by hand." We dipped our hand into warm water and then quickly took it out and splattered it over the clothing. We rolled the "sprinkled" clothes and let them set for an hour for the dampness to penetrate.

We ironed with flat irons that were heated on the stove. The first irons were heavy and the metal handles were almost as hot as the iron. It was hard work and just to think of ironing made you sad, hence its name "Sad" iron. Then in 1871 irons were invented in sets of three with a removable handle enabling us to alternate irons and have a cool handle called "flat iron". While ironing with one the other two were heating. When the one we were using cooled we went to the stove, removed the handle and fasten it to another hot one. Going back and forth from the stove to the table had to be done quickly or the garment that was being ironed dried before it was finished. It was hard to dampen the dried parts without spray bottles. Because all the clothing was 100% cotton, if the clothes weren't the correct dampness we couldn't iron out the wrinkles. In the summer we did the ironing on the same days we baked bread using the hot stove for both chores.

We later got a "Coleman gas iron" making ironing much easier. The temperature stayed constant. We no longer walked back and forth from the table to the stove. When electricity was installed we purchased an electric iron.

In the spring of 1942 or 1943 rural electricity came to our area. It was actually the Rural Electric Association, (REA). At that time they put lines across the middle of a pasture or field. The REA went through our west pasture. One day when the cattle came home for water one of the cows had her udder full of milk. We wondered what happened to her calf and began searching the pasture. Finally we detected the smell of a dead animal. We walked toward the smell and found the dead calf in a hole the REA dug in a low spot in the pasture. They decided not to use that spot but they didn't cover the hole therefore the calf fell in. We could see where he kept trying to get out by pawing the walls of the hole but never got enough dirt under his hind feet to get out. Dad was furious. I am glad I was not on the end of his anger. He had the REA dig the dead calf out to make sure there wasn't another one underneath. The REA paid us the market price for the calf.

Home Medical Remedies

I make no assurances as to the validity of the following remedies. There were no hospitals in our area and only one doctor. No inoculations or vaccinations. We relied on home remedies and home nursing. I'm not sure what many of the home remedies were used for. Below are some of the examples of how they survived with little or no medical attention.

There was no cure for rattlesnake bites. If a person was strong they might survive, but if they were weak and lacked the desire to live, they would probably die.

Apply soap or vinegar to ease the itch from mosquito bites. If the bites are all over the body take a bath using plenty of soap or pour vinegar into the tub.

Vinegar applied to a wasp bite takes away the pain and keeps the swelling down.

For Poison Oak or Poison Ivy make a paste of water with sulfur and spread it over the burning, itching rash. Using the paste was very soothing and usually the rash left no scars.

Simply put some tape over a splinter or sticker and then pull it off. This removes most splinters or stickers painlessly.

My folks were told of someone becoming ill with what the doctor called "Mountain Fever." This was before my folks came to the United States. After the lady got better from the Mountain Fever, she contracted Erysipelas (an acute bacterial disease marked by high fever and severe skin inflammation). It was on her face. The neighbors came to help. They grated a raw potato, put some on a cloth and applied it to the infected area. When they removed the application the potato would be black. They kept changing the application until the infection cleared.

Eating fresh fruit after a meal could cause acid on the stomach that in turn will cause heartburn. The only fruit that does not affect *most* people after a meal is apple and pineapple.

Ground cinnamon sprinkled on two tablespoons of honey taken before food relieves acidity and digests the heaviest of meals.

Disease was a crippling factor physically and emotionally. The worst among children were scarlet fever, pneumonia and whooping cough. In adults pneumonia was most prevalent and hard to cure.

Eating pumpkin seeds are helpful for incontinence and can be used as a snack or added to salads or cereals.

When we had the flu or whatever upset out stomachs, and were vomiting, a lady told Mom to give us ice water and give us ice to suck on. After it got smooth we swallowed it. She said that usually when people vomit there is a temperature in the stomach causing the vomiting. She told Mom if the ice didn't solve the problem to give us ice water with soda. If it didn't stop then give us hot soda water. The ice always worked.

Other diseases were typhoid fever which one acquired from polluted drinking water. Spinal meningitis and measles left some defects in its wake, and chicken pox was just a nuisance and miserable but hardly affected anyone until the person was older. Sometimes one developed shingles from having had the chicken pox as a child.

Before anesthetics, if a person needed an operation they were given whisky. Once the patient was drunk they could perform surgery, extract teeth, set broken bones and so forth.

In the summer of 1938 we were in religion classes and a family had whooping cough. The Sister who was teaching us said to the children, "You children have the whooping cough!"

They replied, "No we just have a bad cold." They exposed all of us to the whooping cough and we got sick. All summer we coughed excessively. I can see why the whooping cough was so hard on infants. We coughed even if we were sitting still. When we did exert ourselves we coughed so hard we felt as if we were choking. At that time there were no vaccines for whooping cough.

Andy and his brother-in-law were overhauling a tractor. They decided to move the tractor but had dismantled one front wheel from the steering column. The wheel that was loose kept turning the wrong way. Tom was trying to guide this wheel and had his arms around it and pulled too hard. In the process he broke his sternum. Tom kept going to different doctors but none could help with the pain or give him any relief. He finally found a doctor that told him to buy Red Virginia Dare Wine, not the pink or white and mix a wine glass of wine and a tumbler of milk together and drink it one-half hour before each meal. When mixed together it tasted like a strawberry milk shake.

That brand of wine only came in quart bottles so it was hard keeping it on hand. In no time at all his sternum healed.

Floured water was used to treat diarrhea.

Diphtheria was caused by bacteria. Patients had problem with breathing and could choke to death. Early treatment was to get the patient to vomit to get rid of the phlegm.

To get rid of the odor left by skunks, they burned sulfur.

We baked an onion in the oven and put the root in the ear of a child. This would draw out an infection.

Broken bones, sprains, or other painful bruises were helped by boiling white oak bark to make a tea using one-cup leaves to one gallon water. Three or four times the injured part was soaked first in cold tea for five minutes and then in hot tea for five minutes, alternating hot and cold every five minutes for a total of twenty-five minutes. This will speed the healing process.

Indians used white willow bark in the place of aspirin.

Paul had restless leg syndrome and was told to take a bar of soap in bed with him and put it between the sheets. It took several months to get relief but it worked.

A friend had a seed wart under his nose and every time he shaved he cut the wart off and it bled. Someone told him to put raw egg whites on it so every morning his mother made eggs he dipped his finger in the eggshell and put it on the wart. Eventually the wart disappeared.

A cup of Epsom salts dissolved in hot water used to draw out infection, treat sprains and a multiple of other uses. Sometimes vinegar or soda was added to the Epsom Salts water. Adding soda was wonderful for sprains.

Open Sores

The bulk tobacco that came in little sacks and was used to roll cigarettes is a good healer when applied to open sores or skin problems like eczema. Some people put it in their mouths and chewed it before applying to the sore.

Stable Salve was used for open sores as we use antibiotics today.

Salt pork or ground flaxseed was used for nail punctures in place of a tetanus shot. The salt pork that we used was the bacon that my Dad loved to eat. There was no meat just fat. A slice was put on a white rag because there were no bandages and a bandage would not have held this in place. Flaxseed was mixed with a small amount of water or milk to make a paste and placed on a sore then covered with a rag. This was also good for any kind of sore or cut.

Turpentine was also used in place of iodine to disinfect open wounds.

Colds and Coughs

Mustard plasters were used to cure chest colds by mixing one spoon of dry mustard with four spoonfuls of flour and moistened with water to make a past. This mixture was spread thinly on a cloth and placed on the chest. It had to be watched closely so it didn't blister. Just as soon as the skin turned pink the mustard plaster was removed and the chest washed. The mustard plaster was then placed on the back taking the same precautions. This helped loosen congestion from colds and pneumonia.

We put an onion and some sugar in water on the back of the coal cook stove to simmer and used it for cough syrup. Some people used honey instead of sugar in the onion syrup.

I remember once when I had a cold, I went to the doctor and he gave me a prescription that didn't help. We went back two more times and after the third prescription I still wasn't any better. Mom said, "The heck with this!" Mom decided to make a hot toddy for me. She sautéed a diced up clove of garlic in butter, added sugar to taste and used one part bourbon and two parts water. I drank this just before I went to bed for three nights and by then I was over my cold. One of the secrets of this remedy is to be prepared for bed because the hot toddy makes a person very warm. After drinking this remedy hop into bed. As you start to perspire toxins will be released from your body. This release of toxins along with the relaxation effect offers a good night's sleep and is a great healer. When a person is ill sleep is very important for recovery.

We gargled with hot salt water to soothe a sore throat. Later a neighbor shared another remedy with us. She told us to gargle with one-half water and one-half peroxide every half hour. It sure made a mouth full of foam from all the germs but after about the fourth time the foam subsided along with the pain.

When we had a cold and coughed at night and couldn't sleep Mom rubbed our feet with Vicks, put socks on us and we went to sleep. Rubbed sage can help a bad cough. We would bring a pan of water to boiling, drape a towel over the head to make a tent. We would drop the sage into the boiling water and breath in the steam. For best results be under the tent when dropping the sage into the boiling water.

Another remedy for a cold was to include a few drops of kerosene in a mixture of water and sugar, which was swallowed.

One-tablespoon warm honey and one-fourth teaspoon cinnamon powder taken daily will help the most chronic cough, cold and help clear the sinuses.

Another cold remedy is to take a soaking bath using one-third gallon apple cider vinegar in a tub full of water.

When we digest food we put toxins in our body just like building a fire produces smoke. This fuel burning causes buildup similar to those in a fireplace. Therefore we need to do something to remove the toxins from our body just like we need to clean the chimney. Fresh ground flaxseed eaten daily in our diets, on salads or other foods is one way to help remove toxins. Flaxseed should be ground fresh daily. Garlic is another wonderful toxin remover along with raw fruits and vegetables. For colds, Mom baked a bulb of garlic in a small amount of lard for forty-five minutes and then we ate it on toast at one sitting.

Home-brewed whisky was used for many things and seemed to be a cure for every other ailment one had.

Years ago the prescription bottles didn't have the push and twist lids on them. We never had 'SEALED FOR PROTECTION' on the jars. No one opened a jar that they did not want to buy while in the store.

A cup of oatmeal in a tub of bath water stops rash.

For livestock, when the calves had scours (a bad diarrhea) we put cinnamon in their formula. We kept making it stronger until it stopped.

One of our calves got ticks. Someone told us to take an orange and chop it up in small pieces and rub it over the calf. It was the citrus acid that killed the ticks.

Our Family Gets Quarantined

Paul and Andy contracted spinal meningitis in 1929. Paul came home quite ill from his job. He was so thirsty he put the dipper and water bucket by his bed. We were fortunate none of the rest of us contracted this contagious disease, especially drinking from the same dipper. We never sterilized anything except the jars we used for canning. Paul's condition was so severe that he became unconscious and was rushed to the doctor. Dad said, "The doctor picked Paul up and threw him over his shoulder like a sack of feed and I said to the doctor, 'Don't hurt my son!'"

The doctor replied, "He is unconscious and does not feel a thing." It is unknown if either boy had any lingering effects from this or not because no one ever said. Both boys were hospitalized leaving Mom short of help until they recovered. She was also their caretaker after they came home.

We were quarantined for quite some time and all the children missed school. Because the disease was so contagious the school children were not allowed to bring any books home to keep up with their homework. They almost failed the grades that term. My parents didn't know the English language well enough to help the children keep up with their homework.

The few things that were needed from the store during the quarantine were left at the gate. Very little was needed in those days as the farms were very self-sufficient. The few items needed were flour, sugar, coal oil, vinegar and salt. We didn't pay for the groceries until after the quarantine was lifted. In those days there were only the Mom and Pop owned stores that are still in that community today.

The house was fumigated to kill the disease. We had to evacuate the house early in the morning and couldn't enter it until late that night. All we took with us was enough food to last the day and water was not a problem as we went to the well when we ran out. It was very cold on the day they fumigated the house. We all took our coats and went to the first barn that was built, "the old barn," because there were cattle in there and they helped to keep us warm. We didn't have thermos bottles at that time and no way to heat anything so all we ate was bread and water.

*****

Mary got blood poisoning when a nail cut her hand. We took her to the local doctor. He didn't help so bother-in-law Ted took her to Colorado Springs where she was treated. She soaked the open sore in an Epson Salts solution several times a day and applied an antibiotic salve.

*****

Mother became ill in 1946. She was vomiting. Sometimes she would be okay for a week or more, and then she might vomit every day. This confused the doctor. Finally he found a growth at the intake of her stomach. It was unusual because it was hard as a rock. They closed up the old intake and made a new one. Mom was sixty-two years old at that time. Surgery of this type had never been performed on a person her age and this made medical history in Colorado Springs. The doctor asked that she come to see him once a year. He wanted to see how long she lived after such a surgery but she never went back. I kept in touch with him until he retired. Mom lived to be ninety-six.

*****

In 1941 Ann married Art. He was a roofer, and had just finished a job when he was seriously hurt in an accident. He had insurance and filled out a claim form. In the place where the form asked how the accident happened, Art wrote, "Trying to do the job myself."

The Insurance Company wrote back and said, "This is unacceptable. Be more specific."

Art wrote back with this information. "I had just finished roofing a house. There were 500 pounds of shingles left on top. I climbed down from the roof, hoisted a barrel up using a pulley and tied the rope to a post. I went up on the roof and put the leftover shingles into the barrel. I went down and untied the rope. Since I weighed 165 pounds and the shingles were heavier, they jerked me up. While I was going up I met the barrel coming down. As we met, the barrel hit me on the head and knocked me half unconscious, also bruising the upper part of my body. When I got to the top my fingers were wrapped between the rope and the pulley and that broke all the fingers on my right hand. When the barrel hit the ground the weight broke the bottom out of the barrel and all the shingles fell on the ground. This emptied the barrel making it lighter than me. My weight pulled the barrel up and I went down. When the barrel and I met it hit me bruising the lower part of my body. When I landed on the ground I broke my leg. My hand hurt so bad I let go of the rope. While I was on the ground in pain, trying to get my wits about me the barrel came down and hit me on the back and that broke my back. That is how the accident happened, 'Trying to do the job myself.'"

*****

There was a family physician in almost every town but with only horses for transportation it took a long time to get to the doctor. As the family physician passed away or retired every one had to travel fifty miles to see a good doctor. With modern machinery doing more of the work on the farms the younger people moved to the cities to find work. With the introduction of automobiles and faster transportation getting to a doctor was quicker and easier. With the area so sparsely populated there was no longer a need for a doctor in each town. Cars made transportation easier for people in the rural areas to get to the doctor. Limon has a clinic with several doctors and there was a small hospital in Hugo and another in Flagler. For a person living in Matheson, the distance to Colorado Springs was thirty-five miles further than Hugo in the opposite direction and Flagler was further. There are many specialists in Colorado Springs plus a larger variety of shopping stores and cheaper groceries.

Hoover's Dollar

Republican President Herbert Hoover was elected for one term in 1928. I remember hearing about people walking around and pulling the white pockets of their jeans out saying, "This is Hoover's dollar," meaning their pockets were empty. "No money." Many banks in the small towns went broke including the one in Matheson. My folks lost money so they never trusted banks and kept the money at home in a can buried someplace around the farm.

The Great Depression started in 1931 and the use of sales tax began as some states were looking for new sources of revenue beginning with Georgia in 1929. By 1935 more than thirty states enacted sales tax tokens in order to give change for sales tax. Congress also imposed a federal sales tax on a wide range of products. In Colorado five tokens were equal to one penny. They were made from an aluminum and plastic material. If an item cost $1.25 taxed at 3% would cost $1.2875,

Sales tokens

so when it was rounded up the item cost $1.29 resulting in an unfair profit for the seller, but rounding down was an unfair loss to the seller, too. Now with the token, when we purchased an item for $1.25 we gave the clerk $1.28 and four tokens. If we purchased something for $.75 we gave the clerk $.77 and two tokens rather than $.78. People did not like having to carry so many coins and to complicate matters different states issued different tax tokens. The use declined and tokens were discontinued in 1961.

The depression ended by the end of WWII. By then fourteen states had authorized the use of sales tax tokens or paper scrip as change. It has been estimated that more than a billion sales tax tokens were issued. Even when some state governments refused to use them, many businesses did it to help their customers. States issuing sales tax tokens varied widely. The language ranged from Arizona's practical: "To Make Change For Correct Sales Tax" to the political slogan of Louisiana: "Public Welfare Tax Token" and Oklahoma: "Old Age Assistance."

By the end of the depression the general use of sales tax tokens was over. One of Colorado's sales tax tokens was square aluminum with a hole in the center. Printed on the token was "Colorado Sales Tax State of Colorado" on one side and was written " One Fifth Cent Sales Tax Token" and a serial number was printed on it. There was a round one with a + type hole in the center. The words printed on it said "Colorado Retail Token Sales Tax" with the figure "2" on each side of the hole. A red plastic token read "Colorado Sales Tax Token" with the figure "2" in the center. They were identical on both sides. At that time sales tax was 3% so when we purchased something for fifty cents we gave them one penny and three tokens saving us two tokens, otherwise we would have to give them two pennies. It doesn't seem like much but when you didn't have any money that one-half cent was a big help.

During the next election campaign I remember seeing slogans "Back to prosperity: Roosevelt and Garner." Our next president was a Democrat, Franklin D. Roosevelt. He was elected for the first time in 1932 and for his fourth term in 1944. He passed away before he finished his last term. Vice President Truman took over. After that a constitutional amendment was passed limiting presidents to two terms of office.

During the early years of the depression officials believed prices were down because farmers were still producing too many commodities like hogs, cattle, cotton, milk and grain. The solution proposed in the Agricultural Adjustment Act (AAA) of 1933 was to reduce the supply.

In the late spring of 1933 the federal government carried out "emergency livestock reductions." Across the nation six million hogs were purchased from desperate farmers. In the south one million farmers were paid to plow over ten million acres of cotton.

Some of the livestock were simply shot and buried in deep pits. Farmers hated to see all this go to waste after working so hard. It was a bitter pill for many farmers to swallow when many people were going hungry. The AAA payments saved many farmers from bankruptcy. It became the main source of income for many years. The basic government approach of supporting farm prices by reducing supplies continues today.

While Roosevelt was in office, he did bring the country back to prosperity or "The good times." He started programs that provided jobs for people to work and make money. One was National Recovery Act (NRA) that involved school children helping the teachers, much like the teachers' aides do today.

The Works Progress Administration (WPA) and the Civilian Conservation Corps (CCC) spent billions of dollars at its height and employed up to twenty percent of the U.S. work force on projects ranging from construction to art.

These projects put numerous jobless people to work between 1933 and the beginning of WWII. Some of these tasks included building roads, installing sewer lines, laying sidewalks, cutting firebreaks and constructing flood control measures. They managed the natural resources of timber, fish, game, topsoil, minerals, parkland, watershed areas and pastureland. The program built many buildings, projects and operated large arts, drama, and literacy projects.

A lot of people didn't like it, but to those without jobs it was a godsend. Altogether more than eight million people worked for the

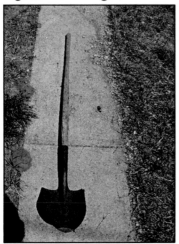

WPA shovel

WPA and the CCC Camps during the program. The CCC workers are responsible for most of our parks today. They got paid $30 a month and were required to send $25 to families back home. They enlisted for six-month terms, and could "re-up" for up to two years.

Men lived in tents and built barracks and mess halls where they were working because it was too far from home for them to travel. Some of the larger projects were building our Red Rocks Theater and fixing up the Sand Dunes plus the lock and dams on the Mississippi River. They restored the fort of "Wild Bill Hitchcock" in South Dakota. These programs fed children and redistributed food, clothing and housing. These men often helped out in the communities where they were employed. During this period someone invented the long-handle spade shovel. With the short handles we had, it hurt the peoples' back. We laughed that they have a long handle to lean on instead of working. Go into a hardware store and ask for a WPA shovel, the clerk will give you a long handle shovel like the men used when working on these projects. There was no welfare in those days and no free handouts.

Everyone had jobs and made money, the nation began to prosper and people were happy. Someone wrote the song "Happy Days Are Here Again" which became very popular and was President Roosevelt's campaign song.

Dust Bowl Years go on and on and on...

Indians said, "White man turn earth up-side-down." How true! He was referring to plowing the soil. The Indian dug a small hole beside the grass and dropped a kernel of corn in the hole then covered the corn, never disturbing the grass.

Mary said, "Mom and I walked barefoot after cows for the morning milking in the west pasture and never got any prickly stickers in our feet." There were no weeds to leave stickers. When I was little I can remember hoeing weeds and watering the garden barefoot. As the farmers turned the soil and built roads, they left the ditches bare allowing the weeds to take root. All types of weeds with stickers grew. The strong winds of the dustbowl days carried the seeds for miles.

Inexperienced and shortsighted homesteaders never used any form of soil conservation. Fields were plowed and planted every year with the same crops in the same fields. The farmers overgrazed the grassland further destroying the land for which they had worked so hard.

In the early 1930's we experienced the dust-bowl-days. The drought lasted for six or seven years. The winds blew hard for several days without stopping. There was little rain for more than three years. When we had those really windy days the dust was so thick it was dark in the house. For us to see, the lamp was lit all day long. The wind was so strong it carried the dust from state to state. We tried to keep the dust out of the house by closing the pull down shades and putting a sheet over the shade but to little avail. There was also a drought in the 1950's, but because we practiced better land management the dust from the field wasn't as much of a problem.

After several days the strong winds died down giving us a break. Those were the days we tried to clean the house. We couldn't sweep up the dust because it was too fine and we would just chase it around. We had to wash dust from the ceiling and walls. The curtains, windows, bedding, the shelves in the kitchen cabinets, dishes and cooking utensils had to be washed. We didn't have vacuum cleaners to collect the dust.

Mary said, "Frank took a jar to the well because we were out of drinking water. To find the well he followed the garden fence line.

The fence was fifteen feet from the well so he was able to find it. He filled the jar, put the lid on and followed the fence back to the house. When he got back the jar was full of mud because the wind had blown dirt in it before he got it covered."

The winds blew so hard and it was so dry that it was difficult to grow much. There was no feed for the livestock. My brothers went into the pasture and cut out the soap weeds. They put them through the ensilage cutter chopping them very fine and mixed them with what we grew. This is what we fed the animals in the winter.

Tumbleweeds were trapped against every fence acting as a wonderful windbreak for the soil. Fences were covered with the precious soil. We had a gooseberry bush and some other plants by the garden fence. The wind covered them with dirt and smothered them. There was a drift of topsoil on the south side of our house and my brothers had to use the Fresno Scraper to drag the dirt away.

To bring the milk from the barn my brothers put it in a ten gallon can and put a tea towel under the lid. When we opened the can there was dust on the tea towel all round the lid. When we went outside we wore handkerchiefs over our noses and mouths to enable us to breath and keep out as much of the dust as possible. That was the only way we could get anything done.

After the dust bowl years we did learn to make deep furrows and do strip farming. We made those deep furrows in our fields from southeast to the northwest. This way when the winds blew from the southwest as they usually do it dropped the soil into the empty row. While this helped the situation some of the nutritious topsoil was still blown away. We planted corn or beans for a width of sixty feet. We alternated and planted grain for another sixty feet, then back to corn or beans. There were thirty inches between the rows of corn or beans thus leaving a lot of uncovered ground. Grain was drilled with rows only six inches apart. The grain stalks were smaller than corn having leaves closer to the ground. Therefore the wind couldn't get a good grip on the open spaces between the rows of corn or beans thus stopping some of the erosion. After the feed was cut from the drilled area there was stubble left for a ground cover.

The wind still shifted the soil for many, many years, even after all our efforts to stop the erosion. There was a field a quarter mile south of our house and we received more than our share of the dust from it. In the early 1940's Dad and I were coming home and as we came over the top of the hill we could see all the dust blowing from this field to the house. Since Andy was doing the farming my folks got him to plant other crops in that field. Andy was the only one interested in farming and bought the home place. He paid my folks one-fourth of what land was selling for at that time. Andy's son has continued to own the land my folks had and planted it to grass.

In the 1970's the government saw their mistake of having the soil plowed fifty years before. They gave grants to put the land into a soil bank program, which meant that portion of land was not to be farmed for a period of time. They were not to farm the land and were instructed to plant grasses but they were not allowed to pasture it for ten years. The government paid the farmers a certain amount per acre each year to leave this ground idle.

After the dustbowl days it was so dry we were overrun with grasshoppers. When they came it was like a cloud in the sky. They ate everything in sight, even the wooden posts. The people at the County Agent's office mixed a deadly poison with ground grain. We spread this poison in the ditches along the road and in a pasture that would not have any cattle in it for the rest of the summer. We didn't dare put this poison on the fields because it was so deadly.

Grasshopper Poison Spreader

We were up before dawn putting this poison out because the grasshoppers started to eat just as soon as it got daylight. This had to be done early because the sun dried the poison. We applied poison every time a new group of grasshoppers hatched. The farmers shared this poison spreader since it was not used every day. When the brothers finished spreading the poison they washed their gloves immediately. They used the same gloves the next time they were spreading the poison. This was done until frost killed the grasshoppers and their eggs.[18]

Our well was in a low spot so when there was a hard rain floodwater came from the field a quarter of a mile south of the house and from the hills to the east right to the well. At first the stock tank was on the west side of the well. Then they moved the tank to the east side so when the wall of water came after a rain the tank split the wall and it never got into the well. At first this wall of water ran into the lower part of our garden until the dust-bowl-days blew the thistles up against the fence making it act as a windbreak for the dirt. This bank acted as a dam and guided the water to the road where it ran down the ditch.

Fresh Chickens

We grew our own chickens. A setting hen known as a "brooder" sits on eggs keeping them at a certain temperature for hatching. She loses the feathers on her stomach to enable the egg to get heat and moisture from her body. A brooder could sit on fifteen eggs comfortably taking twenty-one days to hatch. Ducks and turkey eggs take twenty-eight days. A chicken could only sit on twelve duck or turkey eggs because they are larger. Mom always used chickens for the duck and turkey brooders because she wanted the ducks and turkeys to keep laying eggs. She sometimes got turkey eggs from a neighbor because we never kept them the year round. We kept the ducks until she had enough pillows for all of us. She then disposed of the ducks and I am sure they went into the oven.

By nature a brooder knows her babies are due in three weeks. When a hen was used for duck or turkey eggs the setting hen needed to be replaced after the first week and before the end of the second week. If the hen was not replaced she left the nest during the last week letting the eggs get cold and leaving the ducks or turkeys to perish.

Mom carefully selected the eggs to be hatched by holding them up to a light in a dark room with her hand over the top of the egg to shield the light from her eyes. She looked for eggs with double yolks, blood spots in them and weak or cracked eggshells. This was called "candling." These eggs could not be used for hatching chickens. The eggs needed to be less than a week old for the best results. For fertile eggs and the best results Mom had one rooster for every twenty to twenty-five hens. Every year she exchanged roosters with a different neighbor to keep the chickens from being inbred.

As soon as the first setting hens wanted to nest Mom got several ready and put a group in the brooder house. In another week or two she put another group to set. Towards the end of the third week of the first group we had to tie the hen's legs with a piece of twine to bolts that held the 2x4 to the foundation. This allowed the brooders to leave their nests for their daily elimination, food and drink, yet kept them confined to their prospective nests and not let them get into fights because a brooder protects her babies. We had a slatted panel separating the baby chicks in the brooder house so they wouldn't get mixed because some hens pecked and killed the different size babies. I was small and couldn't easily crawl over this panel. It was not secured tightly and I accidentally knocked it over on a baby chick, killing it. Mom scolded me but I felt bad enough without being punished.

The next group of brooders would be in the granary and the group after that on the back porch. Mother put a curtain across the back of the porch where the brooders were so we didn't bother them. A hen likes privacy when nesting. Chickens still sat when the weather got warmer but by the time the chicks hatched it was too hot and they left their nest too soon so the last groups of brooders were placed in the cellar. You may have noticed there are never any wild young fowl late in the fall.

My brothers built six small sheds behind the brooder house so the baby ducks and turkeys could be by themselves. This eliminated losing any of the young so the brooder hens could not peck at what were not their babies.

Usually the mother hens accepted the chickens that were the same size as hers and when the chicks began to get feathers the hen seemed to be able to tell which ones were not hers by color. It was hard trying to keep the various size chickens apart so the brooders wouldn't get in a fight or kill the baby chicks. Mom had Rhode Island Red chickens that were a favorite in this area because they had a reputation of waiting longer to start laying eggs and had a longer laying life. There would also be one or two white chickens in the bunch. Mom purchased some Plymouth Rocks that were a speckled black and white chicken. The Rhode Island Red and the Plymouth Rock chickens didn't lay eggs every day. They have a calmer and milder disposition and lay brown eggs. White-shelled eggs have a weaker shell that the Leghorn produces. Today confined hen's lay three eggs per day.

We had a coffee grinder before ground coffee could be purchased. At first we ground grain using this old coffee grinder for baby chickens before the mash was introduced that gave them a start.[19] We purchased bran when it was introduced and soaked it in milk feeding it to the fryers each morning and evening. Bran is the husk of grains such as wheat, oats, barley and rye. The chickens loved it and grew faster on bran. We had to know how much milk and bran to use because as it fermented the bucket ran over. This left a mess to clean up and all the nutritious milk would be lost. We fed some bran to the hogs but it was more expensive than regular grain.

Coffee grinder

As more chickens were needed to feed all the harvesters and Sunday company, Mom purchased an "incubator". This freed us from the hassle of fighting with the brooders and the different size chicks. The incubator was made of wood that stood on legs three feet high and was heated with coal oil. There was a container that held water for moisture because the coal oil was a dry heat. The eggs were on a tray and it had a drop leaf door to pull out. There was a glass lid on the top so we could see inside and Mother could lift it up to turn the eggs quickly every day so they wouldn't get cold. She lightly rolled them under the palm of her hand giving them a turn like the brooder hen did. Mother kept the incu-

Brooder stove and Incubator

bator in her bedroom so she could watch over it. Hatching chickens in the incubator was a tedious job but she hatched 200 at a time.

It was fun to watch the process of the eggs hatching. First we would see a small rise in the shell where the chick was pecking at it trying to enter the world. Then the hole became larger and larger and soon the shell seemed to break in half and the chick appeared. Sometimes the chick couldn't get out of the shell by itself so Mother took her fingernail and gently peeled the shell away a small amount at a time as if it were the chick doing so.

After the chicks were hatched in the incubator we had the brooder-house ready to take them to their new home. There was fresh straw on the dirt floor and a "brooder stove" that was fueled by drops of coal oil. (See picture on previous page.) There was a thermostat that controlled the flow of fuel. Our stove was twenty-inches in diameter with a twenty-inch wide canopy around the brooder that directed the heat towards the ground keeping the chicks warm. It was two feet high with legs eight inches so the chicks could get underneath. We made sure there was no straw under it to catch on fire.

Soon it became easier and cheaper to purchase baby chicks every spring. When we went to the post office in the spring almost every day you could hear the chirping of the little baby chicks. They came in a heavy cardboard box with small holes in it so the chicks could breathe but not lose their body heat. This box was divided into quarters with twenty-five chicks in each quarter. If a farmer ordered 150 chicks one-half of a box was empty. There was usually an extra chick in each box allowing for death in transit. Hardly any died before they arrived. The hatchery notified us by mail what day to expect our shipment giving us time to have the brooder house ready. As soon as the baby chicks were home we dunked each ones beak in the water so they knew where to get a drink as they were always thirsty.[20]

First they were called "baby chickens." When the female chickens became old enough to have feathers they were called "pullets" until they became one year old, then they were called "hens" or "layers." Males are called "cockerels" or "fryers' until they are a year old then they were called 'roosters." A pullet can also be a fryer. A "capon" is a castrated rooster fattened for eating. We only killed the cockerels and kept the pullets for laying. It took three months to get a fryer to weigh three to four pounds. That is why the fryers in those days tasted like chicken and when an old hen or rooster was made into soup it tasted like chicken soup. It was not necessary to add chicken bouillon. The chickens of today have little flavor compared to those chickens we raised on the farm.

When we gathered eggs some hens pecked as we reached for the eggs. Chickens lay their eggs early in the morning. The eggs needed to be gathered every two hours on hot days because the hens sat in the nests while they laid eggs. We always went out in mid afternoon and again in the evening to look for the late layer. Sometimes we found an egg on the roost where a chicken laid an egg before it got up.

Our chickens were free to roam all over the yard. In the spring when the grass was green and the young weeds tender the chickens ate these and the yolks of the eggs were so dark they were orange. When fall came and the grass was mature and brown the egg yolks were a pale yellow. We never washed our eggs because they kept longer.

Sometimes the rains came so fast the chickens didn't have time to get to shelter. It wasn't so bad if it rained for awhile before the hail came but many times the hail killed some chickens. After the rain we went out looking under farm machinery, cars, troughs or any place a chicken could hide. They were so wet and cold we brought them in to dry or they would perish.

One summer when Mom's sister, Aunt Mary was visiting us from Durango, she and Mother prepared some beautiful looking and wonderful tasting chicken. As Aunt Mary set the chicken on the table in front of the men she said, "Here, eat this dead chicken!"

Everyone frowned and said, "Dead chicken? We don't want to eat dead chicken."

Aunt Mary said, "Here Lucy and I went to all the trouble to kill and dress these fryers and you don't want to eat them? Tomorrow I shall bring in live chickens and put the fryers on the table and you can eat live chickens if you don't want to eat these dead chickens. Just look at the time Lucy and I will save by not doing all this work!" That was one of the funniest meals around the table. We scalded the feet and ate those too. There was only skin on them but the joints flavored the soup.

In September chickens begin to lose their feathers and it usually takes four months before they start to lay eggs again. Because they don't all do it at the same time we usually had eggs before the four months. Mother learned to preserve eggs for the fall before the hens were in the "molting stage." She dissolved lime in a strong enough solution to float a raw egg. Lime does not really dissolve; it just makes white colored water. She candled the eggs as she did for hatching looking for the same flaws. She put the eggs in a stone jar in the cellar and covered them with only the brine from the limewater she had prepared and placed a plate over the eggs to keep them under water. This was done in early September when the production of eggs was plentiful and they were fresh. This process was done at one time because when she put the eggs in the limewater and covered them with the plate a scum formed on the top that acted as a seal and was not disturbed until she was ready to start using the eggs. The disadvantage of preserving eggs in this manner was the egg yolks became very weak and couldn't be used if we wanted to separate the whites from the yolks. They had to be used in cooking.

When the old hens were no longer laying eggs we caught them at night and then the next morning we put them in crates and took them to Colorado Springs where they were butchered. There were two ways to check if a hen was laying eggs. A red comb was a good sign she was a layer. Another was by placing our fingers between their pelvic bones. If only one finger would fit then there was no room for an egg to come through. Two fingers were a sign she was either going to start or had just quit laying. The width of three fingers meant she was a good layer. Later we discovered it was more profitable to kill the chickens at home and remove the feathers then take them to the store but we didn't remove the intestines.

Sometimes Mother decided she wanted chicken for lunch or dinner but did not catch one the night before. She looked around the yard at the flock and decided which one she wanted to kill and we young ones ran after it until it got so tired it couldn't run any more. As we grew up there were not enough of us to chase the chicken.

On many occasions Mom got my brothers to help catch the chickens. Here again my inventive brothers decided that was too much work. Frank and Steve made a catcher using clothesline wire. It was long enough for us to walk behind the chicken and hook the catcher on its leg. We were far enough back so we didn't scare it away. They spread the end of the wire so it would easily hook over the chicken's leg. There was a knack for successfully using the homemade "chicken catcher." The trick was to get the chicken up high enough so it couldn't touch the ground with the other foot or they freed themselves. It was impossible to catch the same chicken when we missed the first time.

We always had the hot water boiling for scalding the chicken before we went out to catch one. Mother cut the neck of the chicken just below the head while we held the feet and wings. She didn't cut the head off completely because she claimed the chicken bruised from flopping on the ground. Also, our soil was sandy and the neck would have become full of sand. She didn't like wringing the neck because it became full of blood. After we scalded them and removed the feathers the pinfeathers came next. That was always our job. Since Mom always had her hands in water or dirt in the garden and all the other things she did, she had no fingernails to get under the pinfeather. Fryers don't have pinfeathers, only the older chickens. After removing the feathers we always singed the hairs from the carcasses.[21]

Almost every Sunday friends or relatives were at our house. I often wondered if they came for the food because Mom was a wonderful cook. The harvesters always wanted to come and help us so they could eat Mom's good food and they always complimented her on the excellent meals.

One of our jobs was to look around the stacks in the feed yard for any hen that had laid eggs in any nook or cranny she could find. Sometimes we were lucky to find a hidden nest. It seemed that no matter how hard we looked we always missed a nest somewhere. A mother hen would show up with fifteen babies. She kept them hidden until they were a day old and were hungry and thirsty.

Somehow every summer several chickens would find their way into our garden. They sure could make a mess of the vegetables. Trying to find the hole in the fence where they entered was another chore. Sometimes Mom had us sit somewhere within sight of the fence line and wait for the chicken to find the hole through which they entered because we could not see it. Sometimes they flew over the fence. When they did this we caught them and cut the large feathers from one wing and one-half of the tail feathers from the same side. They couldn't fly over the fence because this threw them off balance. By the time their feathers grew out the garden season was over.

Once a year we would be missing up to one hundred chickens. This usually happened when the nights were still warm before we mixed the young chickens with the old in late summer. Whoever was stealing them never knew where we kept the young chickens because they always took the older ones. Dad went every night to shut the screen door on the chickens to keep the wild animals out. When he came in he'd say, "Someone stole some chickens last night." Chickens roost in the same place every night and there would be a space by the door where the thieves had grabbed them. Even after I left home the folks were still missing chickens. We never caught the thieves.

Chicken is the only animal that is eaten before it is born and after it is dead.

Shopping in the City

In the fall we butchered 500-pound male calves and took them to Colorado Springs to the stores. By selling the calves in the fall we didn't have to feed them all winter saving the feed for the milk cows. My brothers removed the cushion seat and backrest out of the car and put in two head of butchered veal. They also placed cans of cream besides the veal then carefully put the eggs on top. The trunk was full of live chickens in crates. Mom went along to supervise the transactions and purchase the things that were necessary for the farm, the few groceries and clothing.

With the car now full there was no room for us so when we needed shoes Mother had us stand on a piece of paper and draw an outline of our feet. She took this paper into the shoe store and came home with a pair of shoes that fit.

I remember going to Colorado Springs occasionally with Mom. We only used cash in those days. When Mom made a purchase the clerk wrote out a hand written ticket telling us everything the computer tickets show us today. Mom gave the clerk money for her purchases. The clerk put it in a vacuum tube and sent it to the cashier some place in an office in the building. We waited until the tube came back with the change. These tubes were like the drive-through banks have today only we couldn't see the cashier.

In those days the stores had wooden floors. The elevators were not automatic. Elevators had an operator whose job it was to run the elevator. He or she operated it by moving a lever one-way to go up and the opposite way to go down. The elevators were open so the operator could see if someone was standing there waiting to get on. When we got to the floor where we wanted to shop the elevator operator opened the door for us to exit. We just waited as she went from top to bottom all day picking up the shoppers.

Butchering Our Own Pork, Beef and Lamb: No Difference Between Beef and Lamb

The pigs ran free in the spring and summer so they could graze. One year our pigs started to die and finally the vet was called. He informed us the pigs were eating the cockle burr weeds with two leaves and is very poisonous at that stage. We confined the pigs until the danger passed.

When we were ready to butcher a hog, water was heated in a fifty-five-gallon barrel. My folks made a tripod from lumber high enough to hang the animals to be butchered and this tripod was placed over the barrel of boiling water. After the hog was butchered using a block and tackle we lowered it into the scalding water. Block and tackle is made with ropes that wear out, so now they use chain hoists. We put the pig on a special table enabling us to scrape the hairs with sharp knives because the skins were used in homemade soap. After one end was cleaned we put the other end into the scalding water and again placed it on the table. The hogs were always too large for the water to scald the center so burlap sacks were placed over this part and then boiling water was poured over the sacks until the hairs could be removed. Dad liked the hogs he butchered to weigh 300 pounds. His bacon was just plain fat.

Many people think that if the hogs were butchered when smaller there would be less fat on the meat. Not true. The larger the pig the more lard but there is less fat ingrained in the meat. A small pig will have a layer or two of fat intermingled in the pork chops and shoulder roasts. A large pig will have the nice pork chops with fat only around the outer sides and the roasts will have a large layer of fat that can be trimmed. The thin layers of fat that are in between the meat cannot. Each time a sow has a litter she gets another layer of meat in the bacon. The more times a sow has babies, the more layers of meat there is in the bacon.

When a pig was butchered nothing was thrown away. A sharp knife was used to stab the jugular vein because the blood was saved to be used in blood sausage. This method is not sudden death like a bullet in the brain so the pig squeals while bleeding to death. During this time the pig would squeal fighting for life. The only thing that was not saved was the squeal. I guess no one had figured how to save that. Cats meow or shriek, dogs bark, cows moo, horses whinny or neigh, sheep baa and pigs squeal.

After we butchered the hogs the intestines were thoroughly washed turned inside out and thoroughly washed again. The digestive parts of the intestine were scraped off with a dull knife and washed before it was set to soak in salt water. They were ready to stuff with sausage.

To make blood sausage, rice was cooked. The spleen and lungs were cooked and ground then mixed with the rice and blood and stuffed into the casings. They were boiled, stored in a cool place and eaten for breakfast. Later Mom learned to use barley in her blood sausage and cook the blood before stuffing it into the intestine. This was easier to handle and not so messy.

The remaining casings were stuffed with a meat mixture for sausage and then smoked. Before salting the hams and bacons the skins were removed and used in soap.

The pig's ears, snout and feet were cooked until tender and seasoned to taste. The broth with the meat was poured into bowls and left to chill. This formed a jell and was eaten for breakfast.

The hams and bacon were preserved with a special recipe of garlic and salt. Garlic was diced and mashed with a wooden potato masher mixing it with a small amount of special curing salt. Enough salt was added to the mashed garlic mixture to salt all the hams, bacons and shoulders. Mom rubbed this mixture into the meat and then using a wooden barrel she put the hams on the bottom followed by the shoulders with the bacons layered on top. On a regular basis the meat was removed from the barrel and the brine was poured into a container. She rotated the meat making sure the pieces weren't touching in the same place and then she replaced the meat in the same order as the first time. She poured the brine back over the meat. It took six weeks for the meat to cure before it was taken out and secured with twine for hanging and taken to the smokehouse. The hams were hung in the center with the shoulders around the hams and the bacon around the shoulders. The sausage was hung to the outside of the bacon. A smoldering fire was built in the center providing the hams (that were the largest) with the heaviest smoke. During this process the temperature outside could not be very warm or the meat would spoil. The hams could be eaten without additional preparation as this process completely cooked them, even though it was a cold cooking process. The smoking process took thirty days. I do not know what kind of wood my folks used for this smoking process but oh "those hams were so delicious."

The smoked meat was put into the cellar and eaten throughout the winter before the weather got too warm. The sausage would become dry while being cured in the smokehouse but was always prepared with sauerkraut. The moisture from the sauerkraut softened the sausage making it juicy and full of flavor, much better than the ones we buy today.

My folks used an A-frame hog shed for their smokehouse until Dad built such hot fires that the twine holding the meat would burn letting the meat fall to the ground.[22] I remember Dad coming to the house with a piece of meat from the smokehouse covered with sand complaining to Mother, "How did you tie the twine? Look this meat was on the ground!" After closer inspection of the meat they realized the twine had caught on fire. After several of these episodes they built a smokehouse that was high enough for a person to walk in putting the meat higher from the fire. It was eight feet square, with 1x12s for the sides but not sealed tightly so the air could circulate. The smoke slowly escaped out of the building. The floor was dirt. My folks were fortunate the A-frame hog shed they were using did not burn when the twines caught fire. Some farmers lost their meat when their smokehouses burned.

To render the lard from pigs the fat was cut into one-inch cubes and placed in a kettle over low heat. If left on the stove too long or cooked over too hot a fire the lard turned brown and food prepared from this had a burnt taste. All foods were cooked with lard as there were no cooking oils. The largest amount of the lard would separate from these cubes while on the stove. A "lard press" was used to press any additional lard from the cubes while they were hot. [23] The lard consistency was soft at room temperature. Even when cold, it could easily be dipped with a spoon. Meat was preserved by cooking and then placed in a stone jar and warm rendered lard was poured over it and stored in the cellar. The meat kept all summer as long as it was cool enough to keep the lard firm. After the meat was eaten the lard was used in cooking. Cracklings are the cubes from the rendered lard and used as shortening in making biscuits. There was just enough lard remaining in the cracklings to substitute for shortening.

We also butchered a two-year-old steer every year. Dad fed corn to it every morning and night. For the first few days we helped Dad get the steer in the barn. After feeding him the corn it didn't take long and all Dad did was call the steer. He fed him for six weeks. The meat was very tender and delicious because the steer was shot where he had been eating thus he was not tense or nervous. The barn was not high enough for the big steer to be lifted up with a block and tackle to remove the skin completely. After we removed the skin low enough we then removed the intestines. This enabled us to cut the hindquarters off so we were able to lift the rest of the animal up and finish dressing it. Because the barn was so low butchering the beef was an all day job

Lard press and sausage stuffer

The Wells Ranch was five miles from our place. They raised sheep and gave us the lambs that needed "TLC" meaning we had to feed them with a bottle several times a day. They felt it was cheaper to give them to us rather than take the time to do this chore. One incident that stands out in my mind I had gone to the barn and returned with a half-gallon of milk in a syrup pail because I wanted milk for breakfast. As I approached the house with my little container of milk the lambs ran to me. One of them put his head in my bucket of milk and quickly drank it. I was not strong enough to push him away and just stood there screaming as loud as I could. I wanted that lamb to get his head out of my bucket. My brothers were near the barn and stood there laughing at me. My mother came out of the house but the milk was already gone. My little heart was broken as I thought I was such a big help only to have lost the milk. Who wanted the milk after the lamb had its nose in the bucket? We also butchered the orphaned sheep that we raised. Canning the sheep and beef were done in the same manner.

At one time we had three head of sheep that we butchered. While Mom and the girls were canning this meat Uncle Steve, Dad's brother and his family stopped by our house on a weekday on their way to Limon. Of course they asked, "What are you canning?"

Mom answered, "Sheep."

"BAAH, You won't ever get us to eat mutton." Mom continued with her work.

That summer Mom had prepared some fryers and all the trimmings, enough for our Sunday lunch. There were no refrigerators to keep leftover food from spoiling. There were no phones in the rural areas to call and let people know they were coming over or find out if we were home. These same relatives, Uncle Steve and his family, came over unexpectedly. Not having enough food for the unexpected company Mom took Mary and me to the cellar. While we were in the cellar Mom said, "Don't either one of you say this is sheep." We went on up with some vegetables, fruit and the meat. She opened the jars of food, took the meat and heated it on the stove with some onions. We sat down to eat and as Dad was passing the meat he said. "Here is some chicken and here is some beef."

They replied, "Give us the beef. We are tired of chicken; we have it all the time." They ate the lamb thinking it was beef and never knew the difference.

Brothers Want a Room of Their Own

My brothers, tired of sleeping in the same room as their sisters, decided to dig a basement under one-half of the house in the 1930's. After digging a space wide enough to get the Fresno Scraper down in the basement they filled it by hand and then had the horses pull it out. I don't remember seeing anything like rebar but I remember seeing an old head and foot wrought iron bed frame, light pieces of frame from some of the farm machinery, and other things used for reinforcing the walls. They put three beds down there. It was drier than the cellar.

When the basement was built they made a window but there was no screen on it therefore they could not open it for ventilation. The basement was dark so Frank and Steve built another room on the front porch. My parents planted concord grapes on the north side of the front porch and fastened rabbit wire to the eave for the grapes to climb. My brothers built a room on that end for summer sleeping. They covered one of the double windows that went to the bedroom using tongue and groove lumber with no finish of any kind, but they had a bedroom. Those two boys slept there as soon as it was warm enough in the spring until it got too cold in the fall. The moths were terrible at moth season and it was a wonder one didn't get into the boys ears.

Frank and Steve loved sleeping out there except the flies bothered them so they got creative again and built a flycatcher from window screen. It was twelve inches square and twenty-four inches high that stood on legs four inches from the floor. This was just high enough to place a pie-pan of milk under it. They fixed a funnel type cone with wire going up the middle with a small hole in the tip eight inches from the bottom. The flies landed around the pie-pan drinking milk and as they went to leave they flew up into this hole and got trapped in the cage. Frank and Steve's mistake was that they didn't fix a way to empty the dead flies. When the cage became full the flies that were trapped in the cage would walk around on top of the dead flies and get back out of the hole and escape.

The Bull and Locomotive Sink in Quicksand

During the summer of 1937 Frank and Steve were helping John put up grass hay on the other side of Big Sandy Creek. It was a dry creek except in the spring when the ground is frozen and we had snow run off. Then there was a little stream several inches deep and a foot or two wide. Once in a while there would be a low place where there was just a small amount of water all year. Since the creek was so sandy a person could dig twelve inches with their hands and get water. The only other time there was water in Big Sandy Creek was when it rained.

One afternoon to the southwest, Frank, Steve and John saw a rain cloud in the sky. Nothing happened and the cloud seemed to disappear. They never gave it another thought and went on about their work. When it was time to leave the field and come home they got to the river only to find it overflowing its banks. The rain cloud poured rain at the headwaters of the Big Sandy Creek and all the water came rushing down the creek. Their only option was to turn the horses loose in the hay field and walk home. Since the water was too swift they walked up the river one-mile east of Matheson and crossed over on the Rock Island Railroad Bridge then walked the four miles back home. When Frank and Steve didn't arrive home in time for chores we had no idea what happened to them or that the creek was overflowing its banks. We were glad when they finally arrived home safe.

Many people and animals lost their lives in dry creeks like the Big Sandy Creek from incidents like the one I have just described. The cattle drives never made camp close to a dry creek or river. They always made camp a mile from either one of them.

Several years later John bought one-half section of land one and a quarter miles east of Matheson. The Big Sandy Creek ran through his property. After a rain, water rushed through and washed a deep hole in a bend of the creek. Then another rain came and the rushing water filled that hole with sand making quicksand. One day John's bull went to a ledge where the hole had been and took a short cut to the rest of the herd. He walked into the middle of this hole of quicksand and got stuck sinking down to his belly. Hoofs of cattle are pointed so the bulls' hooves acted as a probe letting him sink into the quicksand but the flat part of his body stopped him at his stomach.

When Ruth, John's wife went after the cattle the bull was missing. She found where he was but didn't come for help until after she had done the chores. John worked as an engineer on the railroad and was on duty. Helen and George were visiting from Pueblo. He parked his car on the bank behind the bull and hooked a single tree to the bumper of his car and put ropes around the bull's stomach. Andy was helping and since his feet were flatter than the bull's hoofs he was able to stay on top of the quicksand while he was putting the ropes under the bull. A couple of times when Andy started to sink he fell to his knees making a larger surface against the quicksand. Using a block and tackle they proceeded to pull the bull out. Luckily when the bull's front feet were up he was determined enough to get out. We quickly released everything and the bull walked home taking the ropes with him.

I had been told that back in the early 1900's floodwaters came down the Big Sandy Creek and washed out the approach to the railroad bridge. This same bridge that my brothers had to walk across to get home the day they were helping John. The engineer did not know this and the train ran off into the creek. The locomotive hit quick sand and sank. The bell that the engineers rang when they wanted to warn people of their coming to a crossing was made of very expensive metal. Authorities and other people looked for years trying to find the locomotive because of the valuable material from which the bell was made but it was never found. No one ever said what happened to the engineer or the fireman.

Remember in the chapter where I told that when steam tractors run out of water or use insufficient material they would explode? Here is what happened in September 1907 a quote from the Simla Ranch Land News.

"An explosion of the engine boiler on Rock Island train NO. 5 occurred Tuesday morning five miles northeast of Calhan that resulted in the instant death of Engineer James D Hartman and the very serious injury of Alfred E. Chinberg, both from Colorado Springs. The blast was heard four miles away. The huge locomotive was lifted from the track and the boiler was hurled several hundred feet while fragments of the engine could be found for a distance of one-fourth mile. There was no damage to the tracks since the engine was lifted from the tracks. The body of the engineer was found forty feet from the track while Fireman Chinberg was thrown fifty feet in the opposite direction. Fortunately, the fireman only had some severe burns and bruises about the face and head but he is expected to recover. None of the passengers were injured. The conductor received help from some of the people in the area that heard the blast and they took him to town to notify the authorities."

Coal Oil Lamps: Wind Charger:
Now We Listen to The Radio

Doing the chores in the winter was complicated by the fact that we used one hand to hold the coal-oil lantern to give off enough light so we could see what we were doing. Unless we were extreme-ly talented or very strong we could only carry one bucket and the lantern and had to make many trips to do all the chores.

Coal oil lantern

On the kitchen table we had a "lamp" that burned coal oil. Today they call it kerosene. Usually it was up on a gallon can so the extra height shed more light. When we washed the supper dishes we often splashed water on the lamp chimney and it would break. These lamps and the lanterns had to be filled with coal oil every second or third day, a never-ending chore. The table lamp needed to be filled every day during the shortest days. We did this right after school before it got dark so we could see how much was needed to fill the lamps. If we turned the wick up too high it smoked and got the chimney dirty so it had to be cleaned. We hurried with our chores while we could see what we were doing before it got colder and became too dark.

We got a "Coleman Gas Lantern" that was used in and around the barn. After the chores were finished we used the lantern in the house in place of the coal-oil lamp because it gave off much more light. At that time we used leaded gas in the vehicles and white gas in the lantern and the gas iron. We called it white (unleaded) gas because it was clear in color and the leaded gas had a red color.

In 1937 a "wind charger" was put up on the granary to make electricity with a six-volt generator. It was hooked up to a six-volt bat-tery in the basement. If we used too many lights and the wind didn't blow hard enough to charge the battery we didn't have light. There was only one bulb hanging from the center of the room but oh, such a wonderful light compared to what we had before. We felt we were in seventh heaven not to have to carry the lamp from room to room. There were two lights in the kitchen, one in the middle and another by the stove. At least we could see how to do our homework a little better. Unfortunately, we didn't have electricity in the barn. They also made wind chargers with twelve, twenty-four and thirty-six volt generators. This was strong enough to use things like toasters and other light appliances.

Wind charger

After we got the wind charger we also got a six-volt radio. We only listened to the news for fifteen minutes every morning and then we shut it off to save electricity. That is how long the news lasted. There was no way to tell us how full the battery was so we were very careful because we needed lights at night.

Lightening Kills My Horse, Sonny

Things did not always run smoothly on the farm. Before the cooler was built Andy was going to the well to put water into barrels to take to the field for the horses to drink. The field was one and a half miles from the farm buildings. The team he was driving was just a little excited for some reason or maybe they were not well broken and he didn't have control. The corner of the hayrack hit a brace on the "windmill tower" bending the brace and the tower fell on the hayrack. Luckily no one was hurt. John was in the house eating his breakfast and happened to see the windmill fall. He repaired it while the rest of us went on our way doing our jobs.[24]

We used to buy dark Karo syrup in one-gallon pails very much like paint cans. The lid went inside the pail to seal it. These containers will be mentioned throughout this book.

We not only pumped water when the wind didn't blow but we carried water to the baby calves until they learned where home

Windmill tower

was so they wouldn't stray. We carried water to the pigs, turkeys, ducks and the chickens. In addition to carrying water to all the livestock in need we carried water for the household, washing clothes, bathing and all the other numerous water needs. The tiny tots carried water in the syrup buckets even though the wire handles cut into our hands. Finally we got smart and took an old broom handle and put buckets on it and carried them between us thus not cutting into our hands. I was too small to carry very much, but my siblings put two three-gallon milk pails full of water on a stick. They put the buckets closer to them and picked up one end of the stick and I carried the other end. They had a bucket in their other hand. This let us arrive at our destination with three full buckets of water instead of two and a half because a half-bucket was all I could carry.

When everyone left home Dad went into our junk pile and put together a water cart. We did not have a welder or cutting torch. He drilled a hole with a brace and bit. He used nuts and bolts to hold the parts together.[25] Going from the well to the house was on the level so even pulling the cart was easier than carrying a bucket of water.

We also carried water to all the animals that were confined to the barn because of illness. One year the horses developed "sleeping sickness" causing them to run a high fever. The disease is carried from a bird by a mosquito. A hole was dug in the old barn and water was put in the hole, the sick horse stood in the water. Wet burlap sacks were put on their heads to help lower their temperature. The ones that weren't quite as ill were in the tile barn because it was cooler and the windows were darkened to help keep the building as cool as possible. This barn had a cement floor so we couldn't dig a hole for the sicker horses but we also put wet burlap sacks on their heads. Several head died before we discovered the problem. It took a lot of horses to do all the work, so they were very valuable to the farmers' livelihood in those days. Every one that died was a great loss to us. After losing several horses, more were needed.

We had three two-year old gildings that we broke. Frank and Steve trained two as a team and named them Tip and Tap. The third one they trained as a saddle horse and named him Sonny. Considering the small amount of time they spent with him they trained him to cut cattle very well. As soon as he found out which critter I wanted out of the herd all I had to do was hang on and put my foot on his shoulder or he ripped the clothes off and tore up my leg because he ran so close to the fence. The other thing they trained him to do (or half-trained) was to stop if I fell off. The trouble was he didn't stop in his tracks but he did stay near. They tried to train him to stand if we just dropped the reins on the ground. He got smart and turned his head to the side so he wouldn't step on the reins and walked off. They tried to get him to come when they whistled and it worked sometimes. I couldn't whistle very loudly but I did get his attention. Many times he looked up but kept on grazing where we kept him in the pasture with the calves.

One occasion particularly stands out in my mind. After I whistled, Sonny lifted his head but didn't come. I brought the milk to the house and proceeded to do my chores. Dad came into the house and said, "Your horse is at the barn waiting for you." I made a dash for the barn so I could put him in the corral for the evening roundup otherwise I would have to walk at least one mile from the house to get the calves. In the spring there was a small stream in the pasture so he never needed a drink during the day. If he wasn't too far from the barn by evening he could hear me shake a bucket with corn and came running. Horses like oats better but I didn't have any. I kept a halter on him and if he didn't come by the time I went after the calves he'd let me catch him without grain so I put a rope into the halter and rode him home. I had to hide the rope by putting it round my neck and let it hang down my back because if he saw it he didn't let me catch him. The rope was only long enough for a rein on one side. At least I could ride him home if I found a place to mount him. I couldn't jump on bareback like other people.

One time after a rain I was rounding up the horses for work when Sonny slipped on the mud. We didn't get muddy because we landed on the grass. We were by the salt lick trough where we had salt for the livestock. Livestock need to have a salt lick by the water. While standing there licking salt the cattle kept lifting their legs, scaring the flies away and in the process killed the grass around the trough and this is where my horse slipped. Luckily for me we didn't own a saddle, so when he fell he threw me off and rolled completely over. When he got up I was lying under him. His front feet were in front of me and his hind legs were behind me. He moved and in the process he stepped on the calf muscles of my leg but he stopped and waited for me to get up and catch him. My problem was I could never jump up on him bareback. I always had to get him to a fence, a ditch or something high so I could get on. I caught him and hobbled over to the salt trough and got back on him and finished getting the workhorses into the corral. The accident cramped the calf of my leg and the only way I could walk was to keep my knee bent. The easiest way was to put a high heel shoe on that foot.

One day someone came over and we were going to the barn for something. Sonny was in the corral and having a habit of talking to him. I said, "Hi Sonny." He whinnied back at me.

The people that were walking with me laughed and said, "Your horse talks back to you."

Some years later the herd of horses was standing on a long hill when lightning struck. Unfortunately, it killed two of the horses; one of the team and my saddle horse, Sonny.

Many years earlier my brothers purchased a team of mules from the vicinity of Ramah, twenty miles from home. The mules escaped from the yard and headed back to where they used to live. When they got five miles from home someone that knew we purchased the team locked them up in their corral and came and told us they had our mules. We had to be very careful for some time before they learned our place was their new home. They became handy anytime a farmer needed a team and or a wagon as we always lent them the mules after we were satisfied they knew our place was home and would not run away. When the farmer was through with the team he turned them loose and soon we saw the mules coming home. Then the farmer would not be far behind with the harnesses and pulling the wagon behind if he borrowed one. This was handy for the neighbors who borrowed the team because it saved them time in not having to drive them down the road to bring them home. Horses are different. They won't come home unless they have a saddle or harness on their backs or they get hungry and thirsty.

Those Darn Cows Had to be Milked

As time passed my parents continued to increase the size of the farming operation and the herd of cattle. We had a bull and bred our cows. We also raised the steer calves for butchering and keeping the heifers for cows. When we had fewer cows we did not sell milk. We separated it for the cream or used it for drinking and cooking. We only drank coffee for breakfast and had milk for lunch and dinner. We used cream on our cooked cereal or on the rare occasion when we had cold cereal. Our cooked cereal was oatmeal, cream of wheat or wheat hearts. I have not seen wheat hearts for years. I think it was replaced by malt-o-meal. Our breakfast consisted mostly of bacon, eggs and toast. After butchering a beef we often had steak or liver with biscuits and gravy for breakfast. We were very hungry by breakfast because it usually took us two hours or more to do the chores. We probably worked harder in those early morning hours than a lot of people do by noon today.

When we wanted to drink the raw milk as it is known, we always had to mix it before filling the glass or we got the cream. In the morning for breakfast we drank warm milk from the morning milking but not heated to make it hot. We took milk to the cellar to cool for lunch and dinner. Our refrigeration was the cellar until we built the cooler. Then we put the milk in a jar and took it to the cooler to get cold for our lunch and dinner.

The cream was used in cooking, churned for butter and the excess sold to the creamery. One of the things I remember was when Mom and Helen made pies. After they put the top crust on a fruit pie they took a spoon and smeared cream over it and then sprinkled it with sugar before putting them in the oven to bake. The cream and sugar helped to brown the top and made the crust crispy.

Some unused skimmed milk was set aside in a container to sour. It took five days to clabber. When milk clabbers it separates into what reminded me of very soft Jell-O and whey, a watery substance. The whey was around the edge of the container and on the bottom that we drained off and gave to the pigs. When we cut into the clabbered milk it was very soft. Bread was broken into bite size pieces or mashed potatoes were put into the clabbered milk or it was eaten plain. Mom would also set some aside for cottage cheese. The rest of the skim milk was fed to the weaned calves, pigs and chickens.

To make cheese the clabbered milk was put over low heat being careful not to let it boil, and in ten to fifteen minutes it turned to cottage cheese curds. Pasteurized milk will not clabber. Cottage cheese is made from non-pasteurized milk. This made a dry cheese.

In Europe, and at first on the homestead, when only one cow was milked, what the family didn't drink was set aside. Within eight hours the cream came to the surface. A dipper or large spoon was used to remove the cream from the top.

We used the cream to make butter by using a "butter churn." The churn was a wooden barrel that held four gallons of liquid but we could fill it only half full. It was narrower on the top than on the bottom. A stick approximately four feet long with two pieces of wood fastened on the bottom in the shape of an "X" was used as a paddle to mix the cream as it was raised up and down in the churn. There was a lid on the churn with a hole in the center for the stick to go through. The lid was slightly concave at the center so the cream ran back into the churn. Mom took a small can and cut the bottom out and slid it over the stick as cream still splashed out. This little can sure was a big help. The lid had a grove made on the bottom side of the outer edge so part of the lid was in the churn to keep the cream from splashing. Raising the stick up and down turned it to butter. If too much cream was put into the churn it was too hard to make butter. Mother said, "Sour cream makes more butter than sweet cream." The cream had to be a certain tem-

Butter churn

perature for it to turn to butter. I don't know what the temperature should be but Mother would touch the cream and lick it from her finger. I am not sure if she checked the temperature with her hand and then ate the cream or if putting it in her mouth she could tell what the temperature needed to be. She'd say, "It's too cold we need to wait for a while for it to get warmer." Or, "It's too warm go get some cold water." We went to the well, got water and put it into a tub and set the churn in it to cool. It worked and we had butter every time.

Mother also had a large churn that held ten gallons of cream. She never used it (that I remember). I guess she needed that large a churn when the other children were growing up and made butter for sale. She had a one-pound butter box to make it look like butter in the stores.

Sometimes we didn't have enough butter for our next meal and no time to churn a large batch. In that case, Mother put one-half gallon of cream into the gallon syrup bucket and gave it to one of us children to churn. We shook this bucket up and down and made butter. Sometimes we were too small to finish the chore so the bucket was passed back and forth between anyone who could shake it. This made enough for a meal or two until we had time to whip up a large amount. This was not washed as clean as a large batch because it was gone before it had time to mold.

After the butter was made, the buttermilk was poured off. It was thin like milk and used for drinking and cooking. The remaining buttermilk was washed from the butter with cold water. A paddle was used to mix the butter and cold water. After changing water many times the butter stayed in one piece and had to be mashed with the paddle to get the water through the butter. Even after the water looked clean indicating there was no more buttermilk in it we continued to change the water several more times. Salt was added and worked into the butter. Then the butter was washed yet again. We mashed the butter several times until the excess water and air bubbles were mashed out. Moldy butter was an indication that the buttermilk had not been thoroughly washed from the butter. Fried butter was used often as a common seasoning. To make this the butter was placed in a skillet and cooked until it turned slightly brown. Foods requiring fried butter for seasoning tasted much better than using the pasteurized butter of today.

A separator was a necessary piece of equipment for the house, and folks had one for as long as I can remember. This equipment separated the cream from the milk. There was approximately a cup of cream per gallon of milk.[26] The separator had to be washed every morning. We rinsed the disks and then separated them so they weren't touching each other while they dried since they were metal and rusted easily.

Every five days we washed each disk separately and dried them. We didn't have to wash it at night because the nights were cool and the milk left in it wouldn't sour. Each morning and evening we poured a dipper of water through the separator when we finished. The first part of this creamy water was caught in a cup and was used in the morning coffee or cooking. If water was not poured through the separator in the evening the next morning the cream in the bowl would be stiff. Until the warm milk heated the thick cream left in the bowl the separator didn't function properly. We wanted the butterfat content to be in a good range to receive the best price for the cream as this meant money in our pockets.

Milk separator

The price was the same for sweet cream as for sour cream in the small towns. The rural town creameries usually paid a few cents less than market price because they had to freight the cream to larger cities where it was made into butter. Also the creamery operator needed to pay the local expenses. When my folks went to Colorado Springs they always took the cream directly to the creamery keeping the sweet cream separate from the sour as a higher price was paid for sweet cream that was used in ice cream. We usually had ice cream before we left the creamery but there was no time to dilly-dally because we still had to take the veal and chickens to the store and slaughterhouse.

There used to be a creamery in every town. Mom used the money from the cream and eggs at the general store to purchase everything we needed from food to clothing. Sometimes there would even be a little extra. As times changed there wasn't enough cream because milking became easier with the milking machines so the farmers milked more cows and sold milk at a better price. Creameries closed their doors in the mid 1950's.

Eventually separator bowls were made from stainless steel because they didn't rust. They were turned upside down to drain before putting them in the refrigerator and were washed only once a week. My folks never invested in one of these so each morning we still had to wash the separator. These had electric motors but because of the weight of the bowl it was necessary to start it with the crank. This electric motor kept the speed rotation of the bowl stable so the cream always tested the same. The creamery had a way of testing the butterfat content by a chemical. They put it in a test tube in a tank with a motor that rotated at a high rate of speed. The creamery weighed the cream a farmer brought in and with the testing they knew how much to pay him for his product. When a cow has a calf the butterfat content is quite low so if too many come fresh in a short length of time the butter fat count would be low. For several years after the creameries closed their doors the trains took the cream to Colorado Springs.

A gentleman we knew who worked for Sinton Dairy in Colorado Springs said, "The cream was separated from the milk here at the dairy. The cream was used for ice cream, butter and other cream products. The dairy then used olive oil or another type of oil that they added to the milk to bring the fat content up to the required specifications. The oils and milk were then put through a small tube using high pressure. With this process, and pasteurization and homogenization, the oils will not separate from the milk."

To have more cream we weaned the calves after they were six weeks old. After separating the milk while the milk was still warm, we took the skim milk back to the barn and fed it to the calves. It was a trick to teach the calves to drink from a bucket. They held their heads up to get the milk from the cow but had to put it down to drink. We held their heads in the bucket and dipped our fingers in the milk and put it into their mouth up and down, up and down. The good ones caught on fast but the ornery ones would fight kick and bite our fingers. Once they caught on we needed to be careful because if they saw us with a bucket they came running, thinking it was for them. We no longer fed the calves the skim milk after they reached the age of four months. If we had a runt we fed it milk longer.

The cats always got a large bowl of milk at the barn before we brought it to the house to be separated. They never got any cat food. They lived on what they caught and the whole milk as it was

142

called. The dogs always got skim milk and scraps from the table. Somehow they seemed to be able to catch a wild rabbit to eat, and this was their food. Sometimes it was fun to watch a dog trying to catch a rabbit. When a rabbit changed directions, most dogs cut across taking a short cut saving all those steps the rabbit made doing the circle. Other dogs followed the tracks the rabbit made like the dogs at the racetracks. The stupid dog that followed the rabbit tracks never caught a rabbit because rabbits can outrun a dog. My brothers felt sorry for both types of dogs and occasionally killed them a jackrabbit.

The first milk from a fresh cow (a fresh cow is one that just had a calf) is very thick for the first few days. (The cats and dogs love it.) This milk is important for the survival of a calf and impossible to live without. A cow's milk has very little cream for the first several weeks after calving. The longer the cow has been fresh the richer her milk, meaning there is more cream. After a cow has been milked for nine months we milked her once a day to dry her up and gave it to the cats, dogs, chickens or pigs.

When the calves were small they sometimes couldn't drink all the milk so we milked every morning and night what the calf didn't drink. We milked before we let the calves have any so we could use two hands then let them finish. Some cows held their milk and didn't release it until the calf was sucking so we had to steal the milk at the same time the calf ate. The calf could milk faster with their mouths than we could with two hands.

Some cows were nice and would stand still while being milked. Others kicked. I do not know if they didn't like the process or were just ornery. They still had to be milked so we hobbled the cow for protection using "kickers."[27] We milked twice a day 365 days a year and even on that extra day in leap year regardless. Those darn cows still had to be milked!

In the fall the cows always found the cockle burr patch or some other kind of stickers to walk through and get their tails full. Sometimes they would lie down in the patch of stickers and got them in the hairs of their milk

Cow kickers

bags. These cockle burrs or stickers had to be removed or we got stickers in our hands while milking or they poked the cow and then they kicked us. Sometimes the stickers were so tightly tangled we had to cut them out with scissors. We even had to put kickers on the nicest cow when this happened. When we sat down to milk the cow she invariably switched her tail and caught us along the side of the head. It did not matter if we were tall or short it seemed she knew just exactly where to swing that tail. But still, those darn cows had to be milked!

In the winter the cockle burr patch and other stickers were gone but the slushy snow took the place on the cow's tail. The cows seemed to love to walk through this slush and get their tails full of dirt only to have it freeze. Come milking time and wham, here we go again along the side of the head with the ice loaded tail. A baseball bat couldn't have hurt worse and felt the same. Milking in the winter was a cold business. We bundled up but our hands were bare and not only were our hands cold, the cow's teats were cold. They even froze their teats. That caused sores making even the calmest cow kick. We could not milk with gloves on, but those darn cows still had to be milked!

In the spring and summer flies bothered the cows so they kept switching their tails but in the winter there were no flies for that tail to keep moving and hitting us on the head. I believe it was pre-meditated cussedness. Still, those darn cows had to be milked!

When the grass was green in the spring, the cows always had diarrhea. Their tails would be filthy from top to bottom. The cow would keep switching that darn tail hitting us over the side of the head. It didn't seem to matter what we put on our heads, the manure still got in our hair and on our faces. It was awful, but those darn cows still had to be milked!

To get milk we squeezed from the top down wrapping the thumb and pointer around the teat then wrapping the third finger, next the ring finger and finally the small one into the palm of our hands squeezing tightly all the way to keep the milk from going back up. We used to squeeze milk right into the cats' mouth.

We squeezed slowly on the cow's teat, using only one hand as we held that darn tail with the other hand. What the cat couldn't catch wasn't very much as they were pretty good at licking the milk. Some milk got on their chests. While we finished milking that cow

The cats get a share of the milk

the cat gave itself a bath. When we started to milk the next cow we got the same cat and did the process all over again. It was still fun to watch the cat catch the milk almost as fast as we could squirt it at their mouths. My folks didn't like us doing this. They said we were wasting milk. I think it was because we were wasting time taking longer to milk because we were playing with the cats. After the third cow the cat got smart and said to itself, "I will get my milk after you finish the milking so why am I letting that idiot keep squirting milk on me only for me to have to give myself a bath again?" So the cat didn't come back.

To strain the dirt and hairs off the milk we used a cheesecloth type material or flour sack. Later we purchased a "metal milk strainer" that fit inside the top of a ten-gallon can that used a special paper filter. We still put a cloth over the top of the strainer to help keep out the dirt so we didn't have to change the filter in the middle of milking.

Steve Gets Dunked On His Birthday: We Finally Get A Shower

One day Steve and Dad came into the house chuckling and laughing. Steve was very wet. Mom said, "What happened to you?"

"Dad threw water on me!"

"Dad wouldn't do that to you!"

"He just did. How do you think I got all wet?"

We all laughed because it was his birthday and no one in our family ever got dunked on his birthday. They told us it was an accident. For many years we had a round "galvanized stock tank" that had to be washed of green algae. Steve and Dad were washing out the tank and they were almost through so Dad had Steve hold the tank on its side while he rinsed it out with clean water. Somehow Dad tossed the bucket of water missing the tank and threw it on Steve.

As our cattle herd increased and more water was needed my brothers built a large cement tank. We also had to clean the green algae out of this tank. We used to have to go to the well and dip the

Cement tank

bucket in the stock tank and carry it to the garden. When they built the "cement" tank they used a one and a half inch pipe for a drain that went to the garden. They put an overflow to this pipe so when the tank was full the water overflowed into the garden. We always left the hose ready to run on a row of vegetables. When the tank needed to be cleaned of the green algae we unscrewed the plug, drained the tank completely and washed it so the cattle had fresh water. While we were washing the tank the garden hose blocked up and didn't allow the water to flow so we used buckets and carried water. The garden hose could not have been used because it was too small for the water to flow fast enough. We needed to get the tank emptied, washed, and let the windmill fill it by the time the cattle came home, hoping the wind blew hard and long enough. If there was not enough water in the tank then that meant pumping by hand or with the pump jack.

We always had a board propped up on the edge of the tank and into the water as sometimes the chickens hopped up on the side to get a drink loosing their balance and fell in. This board allowed them to hop up on it and walk out of the tank safely. We didn't have a birdbath or anyplace that the birds could get a drink. The birds were great for hopping on the edge of the tank for a drink only to lose their balance and fall into the water. If they fell into the water and could swim to the board, they had a better chance of getting out of the water or they perched on the board to get a drink.

The tank was too high for the little calves to get a drink so we took a washtub down to the well and filled it with water from the tank for the calves. They were very thirsty and pushed each other bending the tub. In the winter manure was placed round the north, east and west sides of the tank to help keep the water from freezing. The south side was left open. My brothers built a wooden cover over the tank to help hold in as much heat as possible. They fixed boards on a hinge uncovering only the south part during the warmest part of the day or when the cattle came to drink. There was still plenty of ice we had to break. In the summer the board cover was removed. The manure from around the sides was spread over the garden.

We started selling milk during the summer months when the cows produced more milk. We only sold milk from early spring to late fall when there was a large supply. There was still plenty of milk in the winter months but not enough to justify selling. We cooled the milk in the cement stock tank in ten-gallon cans but it was too deep for the lid of the can to be above water so bricks were placed on the floor of the tank. We put the cans of milk on top of the bricks but the cattle sometimes tipped a can over spilling the milk. After losing several cans of milk in this manner my folks built a cooler in which to cool the milk.

A neighboring farm had a house made from the same tile as our silo and tile barn. My brothers purchased it and carefully took them down and erected a cooler with a small tank inside large enough to hold five ten-gallon cans. It had a flat roof and covered the windmill supports and extended towards the tank. The water from the well went into this small tank then through an overflow into the large stock tank. In the morning we took the cold milk out of the cooler before adding the warm milk that needed to be cooled.

A truck went to the farms picking up the milk every morning, and left the empty cans that had been picked up the day before. We had a number painted on our cans to identify our milk because we got paid by the butter fat content and weight just like the creamery paid for our cream.

In early spring when the grass was green the milk tasted like grass. We brought the cows into the corral several hours before milking to eliminate the grass flavor. Then the cows were released into the pasture every night. Early in the morning mother brought in the cattle for milking before any-one else was up. Some-times one of us children helped her. Again the cattle had to rest several hours before milking to try to keep out that awful taste.

The "milking machine" was invented in the mid 1800's but was so expensive and cumbersome no one pur-chased one. They became popular in our area in the early 1940's. One

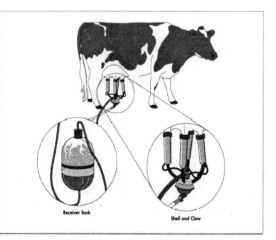

Milking machine

149

person could milk three cows at a time and milk as many cows in one hour as six or eight people could by hand. The buckets were stainless steel and held five gallons. They were very heavy to lift but at least the cow didn't beat us over the head with her tail because it didn't take that long to wash her udder, put the milking machine on and take it off. My folks never purchased a milking machine.

Eventually a "cooler" to cool the milk was invented that sprayed ice water on the cans. The top had lids above each can for the farmer to fill with milk. The front had doors like a walk-in cooler enabling the trucker to pull them out. A mixer was used to stir the milk in the cans so it cooled faster and was made of metal with a solid round paddle on the bottom fastened to a long rod that reached the bottom of the can. It had an oblong shaped handle on the top to fit a person's hand while they mixed the milk.

Then the "pipeline" milking machine became very popular. There were no heavy buckets to lift or milk to strain because the strainer was in the pipe catching the dirt. Milk went down the pipe into a "bulk tank. The pipeline was washed immediately after milking. The tank was built similar to a refrigerator. When the temperature in the tank got too warm, the agitator started to rotate while the refrigerator unit cooled the milk. After the milk was picked up in the morning a member of the family went out and washed the refrigerated tank with a disinfectant that acted as a preservative to keep the milk from spoiling.

After the farmers started using the pipeline milking machine, the milk was picked up every other day. alternating routes between different farmers. The truck driver tested the milk for butterfat content before loading the milk. He measured the weight of the milk so the farmer was paid the right amount for what he produced. In the spring the truck driver needed to watch for milk that tasted like grass.

We needed cold water so when the wind didn't blow we had to pump the water by hand or with a "pump jack." My creative brothers came to the rescue again. When they built the cooler they put in a window through which they could run a drive belt from a tractor or a motor that had a pulley to the pump jack. The pump jack was fastened securely to the pump and was used when the wind didn't blow. John bolted another car rim to the rim of the rear wheel of his car. He jacked up the back end of the car and used the rim as a pulley. This saved a lot of hand pumping.

My inventive brothers were at it again. This time they decided they wanted to build a shower. This would have been fine today but in the mid 1930's we had no running water. The only pump we had was the windmill. Keep in mind there was no refrigeration or electricity.

Frank and Steve put a galvanized stock tank on top of the flat part of the cooler they had previously built that extended toward the big tank. They put a pipe to the other end of the cooler and brought it down into the building for showering. They put water into the tank with buckets in the morning until they thought they had enough for a shower

Pump jack

when they got home at night. The sun heated the water during the day for a tepid shower. They took the end of the sprinkler can that we used in the garden and screwed it on the end of the pipe. Presto, they had a shower.

Drilling a Well and Hitting an Aquifer

John didn't like farming but my folks thought everyone should farm. Since he was the oldest in the family he tried to do as the folks wanted. Even though he farmed, he tried being an engineer on the railroad but couldn't do math fast enough. He worked on the freight trains and they had to give the passenger trains the right of way, pulling over to the side to let them pass. By the time he figured when the passenger train was due to arrive it had already gone by. It was a good thing the other engineer knew how to figure how long it took the train to arrive.

John purchased a well driller. I helped him for several days drilling for water on a place one mile west of Matheson. Every time we stopped to add on another pipe we couldn't get the driller to work because the bottom pipe was in quicksand. We worked very hard and drilled eighty feet more before we quit. It was two hundred feet to the bottom but the quicksand covered twenty feet before we could get it cased. If the well wasn't cased correctly there was an awful sulfur smell but if water was left in a glass for an hour the smell disappeared. It was one hundred feet to water but the water level came up to within fifty feet of the top of the ground. Many years later I happened to talk to a geologist and he told me there is a large body of water that went two miles south of Matheson and three miles east. It went west and for every mile west the water level was fifty feet deeper. Going north the water was deeper also but I do not remember the exact figures.

Aquifers are bodies of water that formed in early geologic time. Once they are pumped dry there is no way of getting a new supply of water. There is no spring feeding these large bodies of underground water. Geologists say the earth will run out of fresh water in the future so we need to take better care of our water resources.

Making Specialty Bread

We made many of our own foods and bread was no exception. Mom said, "Bread baked in the outdoor oven that I used in Indiana had the best flavor." She also said, "The next best flavored bread was baked in the coal stove. And the third best bread was baked in a gas or propane stove. The bread with the least flavor was baked in an electric oven."

Basic Recipe is Used for all the Bread

Have all ingredients at room temperature.

Combine: 3 cups luke warm water, 1 package yeast; after the yeast is dissolved beat in 2 cups flour. Permit this sponge to rise in a warm place until light and foamy. Combine: 1 beaten egg, 2 tablespoons melted shortening, ½ teaspoon salt, 2 tablespoons sugar, and add to the sponge. Stir in: About 4 cups flour. Use only enough flour to make dough that will knead well. Knead and then shape it into two loaves. Allow this to rise until double in bulk. Bake in a preheated 350° oven for about one hour.

Krepya

One of our early desserts was "krepya." Here again bread dough was rolled out to one-half inch thick. Mom cut the dough in three-inch squares. She slit a hole in the center with a knife and put her fingers in the hole and pulled to make a large hole then set it to rise for ten minutes. She fried the donuts in a skillet half full of lard. When it was brown on one side she turned the donut over to brown on the other side. We never had any donut holes. She rolled the krepa in granulated sugar but left some without sugar for Dad because he didn't like sweets. Dad used less than one-sixteenth of a teaspoon of sugar in each cup of coffee. He put butter on his pancake and then sprinkled a very small amount of sugar over the top. He said syrup was too sweet and ate very little cake, pie or cookies. He ate a small amount of homemade ice cream.

Kolachi

Kolachi can be found in some of the stores here in the United States. Bread dough is used to make "kolachi. The bread dough is rolled out to one-half inch thick. We cut the dough into four-inch squares. We put in the filling taking the four-corners and bringing them to the center pinching the bread where it was cut to seal in the filling. Some are filled with boiled prunes that are cut up and others with a boiled mixture of ground poppy seed mixed with milk and sugar. Another filling is cottage cheese with a raw egg, a pinch of salt and enough sugar to taste. The egg held the cottage cheese together after the kolachi was done. We put them on a greased cookie sheet to rise for ten minutes and then baked them until the bread was done.

Mother always made special bread for our Christmas Eve meal. She took balls of bread dough and rolled it between her hands until she had a strip one inch in diameter. She cut them in one-inch pieces and put them on a cookie sheet to rise for ten minutes before baking them. These were called "bobiki." Another bread dish was "lokshi." She rolled bread dough to twenty-four inches in diameter and one-half inch thick. She let it rise for ten minutes and baked it on the bottom of the oven in the coal cook stove. In gas or electric stoves they had to be put on a cookie sheet. She baked these breads a few days before Christmas. The morning of Christmas Eve Mom cut the lokshi in two-inch squares keeping them separate from bobiki. She poured hot water over each just enough to dampen them. She added sugar and ground poppy seed and took them to the cellar.

A starter-culture was used before the introduction of yeast. Bread had to be made every five days or the starter would be lost requiring a visit to a neighbor. The starter was kept in the cellar and when we were out of bread Mom brought the starter from the cellar and it began to rise in the warm kitchen. She added milk, flour and sugar to the starter. Before making bread she took a small amount of starter, put it into a jar and took it back to the cellar. When fresh compressed yeast became available we were told it was good for the complexion and we ate it, but it tasted awful. Either it didn't do any good or we didn't eat enough. We used that for bread but Mom only used it if she happened to go to town the day or two before she knew she needed to bake bread. Then they came out with the dry yeast that was so much more convenient and is common today.

One of the chores was making bread because Dad didn't like store bought bread and said, "There was nothing in this, it is like fluff, too soft." He knew the nutritional value of homemade bread, better than we did. I thought store bought bread was wonderful.

In Europe the mill ground the grain into flour that was whole-wheat flour or whole grain flour. In this country we really don't have whole grain flour. It may be in the health food stores. The part that makes the grain sprout has an oily texture and this part is removed from flour or maggots will develop. Sometimes when Mom opened a new sack of flour we found the little black bugs walking around on the top. The oily sprout that was removed from grain before it was ground into flour had all the nutrients in it. If farmers were not careful weevils got into the wheat that was in storage. Those weevils would eat this oily part of the grain and when they did this it is of no value to anyone. Wheat was sometimes stored for years before it was used so the farmers sprayed it with a pesticide so weevils didn't get started in their grain bins.

Sometimes in the early 1930's Mother was very tired and worn out from child bearing and years of hard work. One day after lunch Dad was complaining to her so she grabbed the luncheon dishes and tossed them on the floor breaking many. My brothers grabbed her and took her to Colorado Springs to visit Kate and later she went to visit Ann in Denver. They let Dad think they took her to Brady's, (a mental institution). As a small child it seemed to me she was gone a long time but I'm sure she desperately needed the rest. Helen was left to take care of the household.

Mother had a "Bread-mixing Bucket" she never used because Dad said, "Using the bread mixing bucket was a lazy way to mix bread." He never mixed the bread and didn't know what a hard job it was to hand knead bread dough. Helen was not strong enough to mix the bread by hand so Frank and Andy went

Bread mixing bucket

to the basement and got the bucket and fastened it to the bench proceeding to help Helen make bread. It had a horizontal rotating handle on the top and was fastened to an S shape rod that went to the bottom of the bucket. To keep the bucket from moving it had a device welded on the bottom that fastened to a bench. As the handle was rotated the S shaped rod went around putting air into the bread dough.

Preserving Food for the Long Winter

Mom dug a hole in the garden after all the vegetables were harvested. She was taught to only put in carrots. Lining the hole with straw she put in the carrots (saving enough for us to eat). She covered the rest with straw and filled the hole with dirt then she put boards on top to mark the spot. After the ground thawed in the spring we dug a few carrots leaving some for later. By planting time the carrots were all gone. I understand some people buried beets, apples, cabbage, turnips and onions but mother never did. Our cellar kept the onions and potatoes.

While in Indiana the ladies taught Mom to can. At that time the only way of preserving foods was the method called "hot water bath," using the copper boiler. Food was parboiled and then packed into sterilized jars and put in a copper boiler completely covering them with an inch of water. We had to make sure the water in the boiler and the jars were the same temperature or the jars broke. A rack was under the jars to keep them away from the bottom of the pot. The water couldn't boil too hard or the jars broke. Fruits required shorter boiling time than vegetables.

We had "zinc lids" with porcelain in the top and by using a "flat rubber ring" around the neck we sealed the jars. The rubbers had a lip sticking out of the side. When the lids got older sometimes two rubber rings were needed to seal the jars. If there was a

Zinc lids

crack in the porcelain the food spoiled. Many times we couldn't get the lid off so we learned to take a pair of pliers and pulled on the lip of the rubber breaking the seal. If we broke the lip before we pulled the seal out we were in more trouble than when we first started because then there was no way to get the rubber out and we couldn't unscrew the lid.

Mom purchased a "pressure cooker" that held four quarts for canning. She learned to use it for cooking her beans and large pieces of meat like hams for Easter.

Another one of our winter foods was sauerkraut. To make sauerkraut, cabbage leaves were layered across the bottom of a fifty-five gallon wooden barrel. Garlic was crushed into a small amount of salt in a wooden bowl with a wooden potato masher. Some people sliced onions into the wooden bowl but Mother never did. Enough salt was added to the crushed garlic salt mixture to salt the complete barrel. A "sauerkraut cutter" was used to cut the cabbage. Ours had three knives that were sharpened before starting the process and bolted on an angle cutting the cabbage very thin. The knives were close together in the center of a board that was three feet long and ten inches wide. On each side of this board another board was anchored to the sides. These little boards were three inches high with a groove in it for a square box to glide back and forth over the knives. This box held the cabbage so the operator pushed it back and forth slicing the cabbage. This slivered cabbage and salt mixture was added alternately to the barrel. After twelve inches of cabbage and salt mixture were in the bottom of the barrel, a child of the family weighing less than sixty pounds, scrubbed his feet clean and started compacting this. They continued doing this until the barrel was full. Every fifth way up the barrel, cabbage leaves were spread over the top of the mixture and then more shredded cabbage and salt layers were added. This process continued until the cabbage was three inches from the top of the barrel. More cabbage leaves were placed on the top to keep the shredded cabbage under the layered boards within the barrel. Several more boards were placed crossways across the ones that covered all the cabbage leaves and then a marble stone was used to keep the boards weighted down. As the cabbage fermented it settled and juice came to the top. We dipped off this brine leaving just enough liquid to cover the boards. A large marble stone was on the bottom and two

Sauerkraut cutter

smaller marble stones were on the top to keep the cabbage pressed down. As the cabbage fermented the smaller stones were removed. The barrel was in the kitchen during the fermenting process that took two weeks. The barrel was then moved to the cellar where it was cooler and kept until eaten. We usually ate it all by Easter. If there was any left Mother canned it. As we came to layers of leaves we used them to make stuffed cabbage rolls.

The sauerkraut compacting process was my job for only one year because by the next year I was too heavy. Thank goodness because that kraut was very cold on the feet. Since I was the baby of the family and there was no one light enough to do the compacting my brothers cut a tree branch twelve inches in diameter and devised a type of "potato masher" from this branch to do the job.

When I was small and if I had a piece of candy in my hand and I saw Mother come up from the cellar with sauerkraut, I would put the candy on a chair and run to her asking for sauerkraut. I still love homemade sauerkraut. It tastes much better than what we buy.

Rabbit Drives Make Money

In 1940 the jackrabbits were so plentiful that skinneries were set up in the rural towns. We drove our car across the road in the west pasture to hunt. The driver used a pistol and a person on the passenger side used a twenty-two-caliber rifle. In two hours we had a trunk full of rabbits. Cousin V. J. Headrick, Aunt Mary's grandson, came from Durango and went rabbit hunting at night. He said the rabbits were in a group and he killed several in one shot using the shotgun.

In some areas the farmers used this as a sport. Some of them built a corral type space in a corner of the pastures using rabbit wire. A group of people started to walk herding the rabbits in the direction of the corral. Using more rabbit wire they made wing type devices that they brought towards the middle as the chase came to a close. When the group began to close in on the rabbits the wings were carried together closing all the rabbits into the corral. The farmers caught the rabbits and killed them, removing the hides. They sold the skins and fed the carcasses to their pigs. Mom cooked the legs until tender and fed that part to the chickens. Of course, we ate our share of rabbit. The skinneries paid six cents for rabbit hides and $1.25 for coyotes.

In other areas the farmers started out with guns at the outer sides of the pastures and shot every rabbit in sight as they walked toward the center. When the hunters got too close together for safety they let the rabbits loose from their circle and started shooting as the rabbits fled. By the end of the afternoon they had several pickup trucks full of rabbits. There were so many rabbits they were eating the grass and the crops robbing profits from the farmers.

The next year there weren't as many rabbits. Frank and Steve made skin stretchers from clothesline wire and after skinning the rabbits they put the skins on these wires to dry. We got an additional two cents for each hide but we had to take them to Limon once a week. The next year a salesman came by and tried to sell a mink fur coat to my sister Ann while she was visiting from Denver. The salesman kept coming down in price. Frank walked in the door and took one look at the coat and said, "That coat is not mink. It is made from Jackrabbit fur." The salesman put the coat over his arm and walked out the door.

World War II

During WW II many things were rationed. We weren't affected very much as we had our own meat, milk and butter. Andy knew how to apply for gasoline and since we were farmers we had all that we needed. Kate and Ted came from Colorado Springs every week just to fill their car with gas for free giving them enough gas to do anything they wanted all week. Coffee was another item. Since we only drank coffee at breakfast that didn't affect us. The media announced that sugar would be rationed. Every time Mom went to the store she bought sugar before it was rationed. She wouldn't let me make anything with sugar but Andy told Mom they needed sugar so she gave him some. Later I found out Andy's wife Mildred had plenty of sugar to make root beer, yet Mom wouldn't let me make cakes or anything saying, "We don't have enough sugar."

Another item in short supply was shoes and nylons. Again it did not bother me as I only wore nylons on Saturday nights to go dancing or Sundays for church. Some ladies used a special paint on their legs to make them look like they were wearing nylons. Nylons used to have a seam in the back of the leg so the manufacturers made a pencil that was used to draw this seam.

Cigarettes and tobacco were also rationed but none of my siblings smoked except Paul and he was not home. Tires were rationed, but the worst for us was parts for the farm machinery. The manufacturers were making Jeeps, tanks, airplanes, airplane parts and other things for the war. If we couldn't get parts from the farm machinery dealer, or wire it together, we went to the blacksmith shop hoping they could solve our problem.

Copper and aluminum was in demand for the defense during the war so the Department of Treasury approved zinc coated steel pennies. The US Treasury minted them in 1943. That was the only year before they started minting copper pennies again. We saved our aluminum gum wrappers because the grocery stores had containers for us to drop them in and they were then mailed to where they were needed.

When the war started there was concern that the United States would be attacked so we had blackouts on the East and West coasts so the enemies could not see where the cities were. The streetlights were out and windows were darkened in case a foreign airplane flew over or a submarine got close to shore. People made sure their porch lights were out and covered the headlights of their cars with material if they needed to go out at night or drove in the dark.

Because of the shortages people figured out how to make foods without butter, milk and eggs. They made cakes, pies, and cookies. Some even used molasses and honey. Since we had plenty of butter, milk and eggs, I don't have any of those recipes.

Cats are Ready to go to the Field

In 1942 the last of my siblings left home leaving me alone with Mom and Dad. Andy planted feed in the field a quarter of a mile south of the house. Mom, Dad and I took the team of horses and the hayrack and went to the field to bring the feed home for winter. There were a lot of mice under each shock, because there was a small amount of grain in the feed and the mice planned to live there in the winter. Dad was on the hayrack and Mom and I were on the ground. When we started to put the bundles on the hayrack, mice ran out. I took after the mice and would step on them. I killed a lot of mice so Mom and I picked them up and stuck them in the corner of the hayrack to take home to the cats.

The next day we got smart and caught fifteen cats and put them into gunnysacks putting them on the hayrack and went to the field. A couple of the cats ran off before we could get them to catch the mice. They went back home. When we got ready to leave the field the cats were so full and tired they could hardly walk, so we put them up on the hayrack. Some of the cats wouldn't let us catch them so we walked home in front of them calling, "Here kitty, kitty. Here kitty, kitty," and they followed us home.

For the next trip we did the same thing, only they didn't fight us quite so much. After several days, when the cats saw us hook the horses to the wagon they came and jumped up. As soon as we got to the field they jumped off and were ready to catch the mice. When we had a full load and were ready to come home they were so tired we always put them up on the wagon. They slept all the way home and then we helped them down because it was so high and they were so full. They never forgot the mice and the hayrack because in the winter, when we hooked the team to the wagon, here came the cats. Those poor disappointed cats!

Bits and Pieces

Almost every town had a fair each fall where people exhibited their fancywork and the town of Matheson was no different. What a thrill when we got to spend a day riding the Ferris Wheel, Merry Mix up and the Merry-go-round or buy Cotton candy or an ice-cream-cone that only cost a nickel. Games cost only five cents per chance at winning dolls, toy cars or other souvenirs. Exhibits consisted of all types of fancy work, quilts, embroidery, crochet, knitting, tatting, garden vegetables, field crops, livestock and so forth. Here in the west we have rodeos along with our fairs for the cowboys to show off their talents in roping, bucking bronco riding, bull riding, bull dogging and so forth. We didn't do any of these things on our farm so we didn't participate. There is an entry fee to enter these events and then a prize called a "purse" for the best or fastest cowboy. The cowgirls' common event was the barrel racing.

Airplane lands in Matheson

Imagine the excitement the small town of Matheson received in 1924 when an airplane landed at the fairgrounds. Since there were no sticker weeds, soap weeds, cactus, telephone poles or high line wires, it was safe for the airplane to land in the pasture. The plane landed where the fair was held. There were few airplanes in those days so this was quite a treat.

*****

In the summer of 1942 all my siblings had left home and I was out shocking grain all day long. Bending over, picking up the bundle, then standing in a stooped position placing the bundles to make a shock was quite a work out. While I was in the field I kept working but no one ever told us to "cool down" when we quit working like people working out at the gym. One of my chores was to go to the pigpen to pick up the cobs for kindling. Remember, in those days we didn't have gas or electric stoves. We had to build a fire to cook our meals. When I bent over to pick up the cobs my back hurt so bad from bending over all day long I couldn't pick them up. The only way I managed to get the bushel basket full was to lie down on the ground and put the cobs in the basket. I did get the job done but I smelled like a pig from lying on the ground.

*****

John was puzzled because the cows' milk was inconsistent. Sometimes the cow had a small amount of milk and the next time she would not have any. Sometimes there was more milk in one quarter than the others. One day he spied her sucking herself. He tried to fix the problem. There was a "calf nose piece" that was clipped into the nose of an animal. It was made from iron and "V's" pointing out so it poked the cow's udder and hurt her so she kicked the calf away. It would not bother the calf from being able to graze. John put this on the cow but since she sucked herself from a different position she could lift this piece up and it did not poke her. His only alternative was to get rid of the cow.

*****

We call them dumb animals but they really aren't. It is amazing how livestock seem to know things. Mom and Dad were by themselves and as Dad became too feeble Mom had to care for the livestock. When any of us went back home we tried to help Mom but as soon as the cattle saw us "strangers" they ran away.

*****

"Blackleg," is a disease that could affect the young calves until they were twelve months old. Air bubbles get under their skin on the front leg. The first sign was a limp. As it got worse they hobbled a few steps, then stopped and stood there with the sore leg in front trying to take the next step but unable to put weight on it. We were told that if cattle had blackleg we could hear the sound of rustling paper when the skin was moved on the leg they were favoring. John ran his hand over the affected leg but couldn't hear anything. He insisted our herd didn't have black leg. After losing several head we had the veterinarian come and check. When the vet took hold of the skin and moved it we could hear the sound of rustling paper. John didn't grab the skin the way the vet did.

*****

Did you know that a pig is the cleanest domesticated animal on the farm? When pigs have to eliminate they leave their bed and go elsewhere. If there is not enough dry area for them to sleep they will pile up and smother each other to stay dry. All the other animals will just wake up, stand up and eliminate right where they are standing. They will also lie down in mud, manure and other muck. Fowl have to stay dry.

*****

Sweet corn had only eight rows of corn on the ear. It was one of my favorite foods. I thought it tasted better that any sweet corn today. One ear of corn was enough to fill us up. Now I can eat three. The cob wasn't much more than an inch in diameter.

*****

When we washed dishes we never used soap. I do not know how they ever got clean. We never rinsed the dishes just dried them with a tea towel.

*****

Vinegar and peanut butter were in bulk in fifty-five gallon wooden barrels at the stores. Mom had a stone one-half gallon jug for vinegar. When it got empty we took it to the store to get it refilled. There was a plug at the bottom of the barrel and it had a wooden faucet that they drove into this plug pushing it into the barrel. They used a piece of material over the funnel to strain the vinegar. In the summer there were flies around the vinegar. We also took our jar into the store for peanut butter. Using a spoon they filled our jar and charged by the pound. It was very delicious.

*****

A cow swallows her food without chewing it. When she rests, she regurgitates this coarse food from her first stomach. She does what is called "chewing her cud" which moves the food to her second stomach chewing each bite thirty-two times. If we chewed our food as well as the cow we would be much healthier.

*****

Desserts were reserved for Sundays with the one exception. During harvest time we had them every day. If a birthday fell during the week it was celebrated on Sundays with a cake. Helen always did the baking because Mary and I were too young. I did love scraping the mixing bowls after Helen poured out the cake or finished frosting it. Sometimes Mom helped with the baking, but it seemed she was always running around doing other things.

*****

The owner of the section across the road from us had sheep but no water so arrangements were made for them to come to our place to drink. There were several "V" shaped wooden troughs made from 2x12s and every time they came to drink we took turns at the "pump handle" pumping water unless the wind was blowing. I was too small at that time to help.

*****

When I was five years old, Mom, Dad, Kate and I went to Durango, Colorado to visit Mom's sister Aunt Mary. Kate had a 1931 Model A Ford with a rumble seat where Dad and I sat. One day they ran out of milk and Aunt Mary asked her youngest, (she was six years older than me) to go to the store. They told me, "She is going to milk a cow." I went with her, expecting her to milk a cow like we did on the farm. What a surprise! She went to the store and purchased the milk. The only place I knew milk came from was a cow. On the way home Dad wanted to take a longer route so we spent the night in a hotel.

*****

By 1942 all my siblings left home leaving me with Mom and Dad. We had a dog that we named "Rover." When he was a puppy he was always into things. We would shout at the dog, "Hey You, get out of there," or "Hey You stop that," or whatever the dog was doing wrong. Therefore the dog learned his name as "Hey You" instead of Rover.

We hired a truck to haul our cattle to market. One of the truckers was helping us chase the cattle into the truck. The other man was by the truck helping to get the cattle up the ramp, fortunately so was the dog, wanting to be helpful. We hollered at the dog and shouted, "Hey you, get out of there." We were hollering at the dog, but the gentleman by the truck thought we were shouting at him. When more cattle got to the truck but wouldn't go in the man by the truck walked over and was trying to prod the cattle. Again the dog was trying to help him. When the dog was up by the truck we couldn't get the cattle to go up to the ramp from the back of the corral so again we shouted, "Hey You, I said get out of there." This time the man by the truck really backed away. We were very embarrassed and apologized to the man explaining to him that the dog's name was Hey You. We never made the mistake of naming another dog Hey You.

*****

A "feed yard" is a fenced in place where all the feed is stored in the fall near the barn so it was easy to get to in winter. The fence had to be sturdy to keep the cattle from breaking in and getting to the feed stacks. The cattle could destroy a lot of feed in a short length of time.

Manure spreader

*****

When we cleaned the barn or the corral we put all the manure on a pile. To utilize everything possible and keep the place clean we purchased a "Manure Spreader" with sides one foot high to hold in the manure.

There was a wooden seat clamped to the sides in the front for us to sit on going to the field thus keeping us above the smell.[28] This was the fertilizer we used. Today if this was put in the fields it would just stay there. The chemical fertilizers that are used today have killed all the little bacteria bugs that used to decompose the manure fertilizer.

*****

After Dad died Mom lived ten years with Kate and nine with Helen. Mom spent at least two weeks with Mary, Ann and me three times a year. During the winter months Helen often had a jigsaw puzzle out with which to spend their time. She began to find pieces of puzzles put together that weren't the correct colors, even though they fit. She was wondering how these pieces got there. Then one day she saw Mom walk by, stop and find a piece that fit and put it into the puzzle even though it was the wrong color. She was the guilty person but to her, it fit. She didn't know anything about jigsaw puzzles.

*****

We used to play a card game called "Donkey." We put one less teaspoon in the center of the table than there were players. The dealer dealt four cards to each person. The point was to get four of a kind. The dealer picked up the first card from the deck and if it didn't match what was in their hand they placed it face down on the table and handed it to the next person. The dealer picked up another card and did the same while the other players handed the cards they couldn't use on to the next person. The person who got four of a kind first, picked up a spoon and then everyone made a grab for a spoon. Whoever didn't have a spoon got a letter starting to spell the word Donkey. The person that spelled Donkey first, lost the game. Some people called this game "Spoons."

*****

We had fruit trees in our garden consisting of an Italian plum tree, a Jonathan apple tree and an apple tree from some seed that Paul planted. The apples on this tree were very hard and kept in the cellar all winter. There were four bing cherry trees and twelve pie cherry trees known as acerola cherries. Some relatives and friends of my folks that came from the same town in Europe would come over and pick cherries themselves because there were more than we could use. If Mom had known that the acerola cherries were good for pain she would have used more.

*****

We had a "galvanized washtub" for our slop in the back porch in the summer, but in the winter it was too cold so we brought it into the kitchen. This is the same kind of tub we used for washing clothes and taking a bath. We poured our dishwater in it and table scraps for the pigs to eat. Dad always felt he had to let the ground grain soak, so this also was in there. When he fed the hogs, he put more grain in the tub to soak every morning and evening.

Our bathroom was the outhouse and for bathing we used a round thirty-six-inch in diameter "galvanized" washtub like the one Dad used for slop. When we sat in the tub it was almost Indian style. Our knees were up because the tub was so small. We only bathed and washed our hair once a week, usually on Saturdays. In the mid 1940's we bought an "oblong bathtub" that we sat in and stretched out our legs instead of sitting with the knees bent. It was small and similar to the claw footed porcelain tubs and used more water. Several people

Galvanized bath tub

took a bath in the same water because we were tired of carrying water and didn't have enough hot water.

*****

Folk's first phonograph played records shaped like a tube. The needles ran in groves on the record as the tube went around. The tubes wore out and couldn't be used so the player was stored in the hayloft. In the house we had a phonograph with a cabinet that played seventy-eight rpm records also using needles. There were some Slovak records but without a radio I don't know how we kept up with the popular songs. Ann, Kate and John kept up with them so we knew what to buy. Later we had one in the milk barn like the one in the house that we played while milking cows.

78 RPM Record

Phonograph record player

*****

Mary got married when I was in my freshman year of high school so Mother said to me, "I am not going to send you to high school any more. You will just get married like Mary did, so I see no need for you to go." I was crushed. I wanted to go to high school and become a nurse. Later in life I got a GED and a degree in accounting.

*****

One year Mom planted some different watermelon seeds but they looked like the ones with the red meat. We do not know where she got them. When they were ripe she brought one in. Mom could tell when the melons were ripe by the looks of the stem and vines. When she cut into it, it looked green. She gave it to the chickens and went into the garden and brought in another. When she cut it, it also looked green so she gave that one to the chickens. She went back to the garden for another one but when she cut it, it also looked green. She was confused. She couldn't understand why the indications from the outside showed the watermelons should be ripe. She decided to taste it. It was very sweet. The meat in these watermelons was yellow! The watermelons with the yellow meat do not keep like the red ones and that is one of the reasons they are seldom seen. They are ripe earlier in the season than the watermelon with the red meat.

*****

When we were small, Mary and I wanted to surprise Helen on her birthday. There were some old cake pans that we played with so we went into the garden and made mud-pies. When they dried we took them out of the pans and made them look like a layered cake. The soap weeds are in bloom in June so we decorated the cake with the blossoms. We took our mud cake to the house. We didn't dare take the dirt inside so we asked Helen to come out and gave her the mud cake and sang Happy Birthday. At her eighty-ninth birthday party we again celebrated her birthday by making her a mud cake and writing a poem about her first mud cake.

*****

During social gatherings some people played music. Musically talented people used the washtub as a drum. The washboard was strummed like a guitar. Teaspoons were also used for keeping rhythm. Saws were used to make the melody. The handle was held between the knees while the other end was held with the hand. The player tapped the saw with something medal while bending it up and down. They used different size jugs by blowing across the tops making the melody in the same way as one uses different size bells. Water glasses filled with different amounts of water and tapped with a spoon also made the melody.

After Ann moved to Denver she learned to play the Hawaiian guitar but had to read notes. John and Steve played musical instruments "by ear." They never learned to read notes or had the opportunity to play together. John played the violin and left home before Steve started to play. Steve played the harmonica and guitar. Steve couldn't hold the harmonica and strum the guitar at the same time so my inventive brothers were at it again. Frank and Steve took clothes line wire and put it across Steve's back, then over his shoulders and down the front of his chest coming back up to his mouth. They twisted the wire around the ends of the harmonica to hold it. Today this type of device can be purchased. Too bad they didn't get a patent on their invention.

*****

There was a shaving cream called "Burma Shave." For advertisement they had signs along the highway, most of them pertained to driving. Following are some of them,

At intersections
Look each way
A harp sounds nice
But it's hard to play
"Burma Shave"

The one who drives
When he's been drinking
Depends on you
To do his thinking
"Burma Shave."

Drove too long
Driver snoozing

What happens next
Is not amusing
"Burma Shave."

Both hands on the wheel
Eyes on the road
That's the skillful
Driver's code
"Burma Shave."

Is he lonesome?
Or just blind
That fellow following
So close behind
"Burma Shave."

*****

Magpies are very annoying and one of the smartest birds. They make the strongest nests and are very hard to shoot with a gun. Just as soon as we stepped out with the gun they flew away. The reflection of light on the barrel of the gun scared them away. To get rid of magpies we took a shinny pipe or something that reflects the sun and put it in the yard. They all disappeared. Sometimes they will sit on the backs of the livestock right in front of the tail and start to peck until they have bored a hole through the skin and then eat the flesh. Once they start eating on the animal we put it in the barn until the sore healed. This was a serious problem for the range cattle because they were only checked once a week.

*****

Raccoons were also annoying. We had a piece of hog wire we used as a screen door on the chicken house. The raccoon crawled up the side of the chicken house and got into a hole at the top. We could see where the raccoon crawled up the side. They killed the chicken and would drag it to the door, because they will never be caught in the building. Then they crawled back outside so if we stepped outside with a gun they were free to run, in the meantime they ate what they wanted. They could not drag the chicken through the wire. The next morning there would be a partially eaten chicken by the door. After losing several chickens like that we made a good screen door on the chicken house.

*****

One night our dogs were barking and barking. We went to investigate. They were barking in a haystack at a raccoon between the bales. Frank took a pitchfork and poked the raccoon in the skin. He was afraid to try to pull the raccoon out for fear it would get away. Steve held the fork and the coon to the bale while Frank went to get the gun. He removed a bail and shot the raccoon. He was afraid he would start the haystack on fire by shooting into the stack without removing the bale but everything turned out OK.

*****

Speaking of wild animals, don't ever, and I mean ever let a skunk get to your chickens. I don't know how many they could kill in one night but they just suck the blood from their combs. They don't eat them. One night a skunk got into a little shed where we had about six chickens. I was on my way to the outhouse when I heard the chicken squawking. The skunk was on his last chicken.

*****

Many times we only had three or four cows to sell. Sometimes they were too old or were too mean. Buyers that traded in livestock went to all the neighboring farms purchasing cattle. Mom took them out into the herd and told them the ones she wanted to sell. She seemed to know which ones were not the best as a mother or milk producer.

Even when my brothers got older I remember Mom was the one who always promoted the sales. After the sale of the cattle, arrangements were made for a truck to come and pick them up. Later, there were central locations in the larger towns that were called "Sale Barns". The farmers went there to buy or sell cattle, horses, pigs, sheep and even fowl. Sometimes you could even find pets someone wanted to make sure had a good home.

The buyers teased saying they wanted to buy small children like me and wanted to buy me. Of course Mom said, "Yes, I would sell her." That wasn't so bad except she started threatening to sell me. I was scared. Now I know she would never have done that. And as I look back that was her fierce way of disciplining me. After having fourteen babies and who knows how many miscarriages she was tired.

*****

At one time our herd of milk cows became so large more pasture was needed. They were a mixture of Roans, Reds and Herefords. The closest available pasture was a section of land three-fourths of a mile south and one mile west of the home place. It was Steve's job to herd the cattle taking them to the pasture every morning and bringing them home every night to be milked. On some evenings he had to walk over three miles to the far end of the pasture to round up the cattle. Steve got so tired of walking he jumped on the back of the last animal, which of course made it walk faster. He then got off and waited for the last animal and jumped on that one's back. He continued this until he arrived home. He was very lucky that they did not decide to buck or stampede.

When the party owning the section of grass across the road wanted to sell my folks purchased it saving Steve all those miles of walking every morning and night. Now we only had to walk two and a half miles at night rounding up the cattle for milking. Later that became the job for Mary and me.

*****

Today the dairy herds are Holsteins that are heavy milk producers but their milk isn't as rich as that of other breeds. If the Holstein does not give at least five gallons of milk per milking then she is not considered a good cow for the dairy to keep. Our range cattle were also our dairy herd, a dual-purpose mixture of roans, reds and white faces. Today most farmers specialize and their range cattle are beef cattle consisting of Herefords, Black Angus and Charlottes in this part of the country. These range cattle only produce enough milk for the baby calf to survive until it is old enough to eat grass.

*****

The door to the outhouse was usually facing the house although I'm not sure why. Our outhouse door was on the south so in the wintertime if a person chose to do so on nice days and it was during the noon hour we could leave the door open and enjoy the sun. The toilet tissue was from a Wards or Sears catalogue. On some occasions we used a corncob or straw if we were away from the outhouse. Our outhouse had two large holes for the adults and two small holes for the little ones. Oh, was it ever cold in the winter with the wind howling during a blizzard. That was miserable!

A hole was always dug for the waste. When the hole was almost full another hole was dug covering the remainder of the first hole with dirt and putting the outhouse over the new hole. We had to make sure the new hole was not where the last one had been.

One of the things the Halloween pranksters loved to do was push over the outhouses. One year we had several teenagers helping with some odds and ends on the farm. The day after Halloween the Smith boy didn't come to work. The other boys claimed they didn't know where he was. Later we found out that while the boys were pulling their pranks around town the Smith boy forgot to watch and when he pushed on an outhouse his foot slipped and he fell into the hole. He smelled too bad to come to work.

Another common prank on Halloween was to roll trash barrels into the streets. Propane, similar to natural gas became popular in our area after the war and became the main source of fuel so people burned their trash in fifty-five gallon open barrels in their backyards. One thing that could be counted on was the pranksters rolling out the barrels. A person had better be smart and make sure his trash barrels were empty on Halloween or the owner was picking up trash all over his yard.

*****

We always worked from the right side, whether milking them or putting on the milking machines. For horses we work from their left side; putting on the saddle, mounting to ride or harnessing them.

*****

When I was a young girl Mom put lard on my hair. It wasn't dry and flighty. We washed our hair once a week with a bar of soap. I never used shampoo on my hair until I was fifteen years old. Mom also greased her hands with lard in place of using hand lotion.

*****

The homestead was on the north side of the tracks and the home place was on the south. When the folks moved to the home place, they still used coal that fell off the railroad cars. Mom sent John and Kate to pick up the coal. She needed to stay home and take care of the new babies and help Dad with the farming. She'd say, "John and Kate, it is time for the two of you to go to the railroad because the train will soon go by." When the fireman on the train saw the children picking up lost coal he shoveled more off for them. They put the coal into a sack and carried it home between them. This was their fuel for many years. Mom still took the team and wagon and went to The Big Sandy Creek for wood from the cottonwood trees or the tracks for railroad ties.

*****

When we were out in the field and got thirsty and stopped for a drink of water, we always had someone pour cold water on the back of our hands or on the inside or our wrists before we took a drink. If we followed this procedure, it would keep us from going into shock, because it was very hot in ninety-five to 100 degree weather and we were working in the sun. Our cool water was a gallon glass jug with a burlap sack wrapped around it and dampened with water. As the breeze blew on the jug the wet sack worked like an air conditioner. The water was as cold as the water we take from the refrigerator today.

The jugs we used for water in the fields in the summer got dirty and often needed to be cleaned. Mom would have me go outside and pick up some small pebbles from the dirt in the yard. These pebbles needed to be about the size of marbles. She put these pebbles into a jug with some water and would shake it. This would clean the jug. There were no brushes that will go into a gallon jug and get around the curve at the neck for cleaning. When I was small Mom would have one of the other children shake the jug. When I got big enough she had me shake the jug. The soil was sandy and finding pebbles was a chore so one time I decided I would just put in a hand full of dirt. It did not work. I had mud. What a mess!

One fall the boys lost a jug of water in the field that was half full. We didn't go looking for it. The next spring when they went to the field they found it. We were surprised it did not freeze and break over the winter months. When it fell off the piece of machinery it landed on its side. When it froze in the winter there was plenty of room for the water to expand.

*****

Mary was working at the laundry in Ft. Carson. Occasionally the ladies she worked with brought something extra in their lunch to share with the other ladies. During lunch one day while they were eating, the conversation came around to oxtail soup. Pat said, "You won't ever get me to eat oxtail soup."

Jane said, "Just you watch, I am going to bring some oxtail soup and Pat will eat it."

Several weeks later Jane came to work with a little extra soup she made the night before and said to Mary, "I brought some oxtail soup today but don't tell Pat what I brought."

During lunch while everyone was eating, Pat said, "This is the best beef soup I have ever eaten."

Jane and Mary could hardly keep from laughing. They never told Pat that she ate oxtail soup.

*****

My sis came from Portland, Oregon with her two year old son. She visited all her siblings so her son drank the local well water at each place they visited. He developed a case of diarrhea so bad he just screamed. Ann took him to the doctor who told her to give him a diet of soda crackers and bananas.

*****

I was told to put a drop of Jasmine oil and a drop of lavender oil on a piece of cotton and put it in my pillow case every night. If I woke up during the night it would help me go back to sleep rather than lay there for hours.

*****

A friend told me that if you sprinkle cinnamon around your sleeping bag snakes and bugs will not cross this line because the cinnamon burns their stomach. This is supposed to work for anything that crawls on its stomach.

The End

Epilogue

My folks continued to live on the farm where Mom had cattle, pigs and chickens until Dad developed Alzheimer's. One blizzard day Mom was out taking care of the livestock and on her way to the house she saw a dark object in the blizzard. When she couldn't find Dad in the house she suspected what she saw in the snow was Dad. She went in that direction and hollered for him. When he answered she found him and brought him back into the house. For the rest of the winter Mom locked him inside the house on bad days. During the fall of 1961 Mom gave the livestock to Andy and she and Dad moved to Colorado Springs with Kate. Dad passed away the next spring on March 20, 1962 at the age of eighty-seven. Mother remained with Kate for ten years. She then moved to Pueblo and lived with Helen for nine more years until her death at the age of ninety-six on March 1, 1981.

Most of the buildings on the home farm are now gone except the silo, tile barn, house, windmill tower and milk cooler. The old barn is starting to sag.

Today the town of Resolis is abandoned. There are no streets, not even a house or marker, even though it is still on the map. The only way I knew I was at the site of Resolis was where the road crossed the old railroad bed. The Rock Island Railroad is no longer in business and all the tracks have been removed. Now there is a path where the tracks were from town to town between Limon and Colorado Springs.

I was the last one to move away and my siblings had gone on with their lives. I helped Mom and Dad. In 1945 I married Tom Cirbo who was in the Army. After our wedding on December 1st, we went to Ft Ord, Ca. He was sent to Korea and I moved back home. We continued to live with Mom and Dad until 1947. We moved just east of Matheson and I took care of them until they moved to Colorado Springs in 1961.

[1] A harrow had ten-inch spikes pointing toward the ground and was used as a rake to cover the seeds. If a heavy rain fell it crusted the ground and the seeds couldn't sprout. Mom took the harrow and broke the crust allowing the seeds to pop up. A section of a harrow has six rods thirty inches long spaced six inches apart. The spikes were bolted six inches apart in an uneven fashion so they moved the ground in different places. They were bolted two inches above the rods, so as the spikes wore down they could be lowered. One horse pulled one section. There was a lever, so when it wasn't needed we moved the spikes to the back so it just glided over the land. We walked behind the harrow. After we got a lister we also got harrows just wide enough to fit down in the furrow to loosen the soil for corn and beans.

[2] The wagon box was eight feet long and two feet wide. There were two 1x12s placed vertically around the sides for holding the grain, (pronounced one by twelve's meaning a board is one inch thick and twelve inches wide and can be of any length. The same goes for a 2x4 meaning the board is two inches thick and four inches wide and can be of any length). The top board had a piece of metal strip fastened to the bottom between the two boards to keep the grain from falling out. The wagon box fit on the same frame as the hayrack so my folks had only one set of wheels for the two pieces of equipment.

[3] A lot of homes had only two rooms. Some were built with three rooms in a row. The two and three room homes sometimes had more rooms added. Most were twenty-six or twenty-eight feet square. My folks built a thirty-two foot square house with four-rooms and an eight-foot front porch across the length of it. They later added a back porch the length of the house eight feet wide. The frame of the house was made of 2x4s spaced twelve inches apart. Most houses were made of 2x4s spaced eighteen inches apart.

[4] The crowbar was a solid piece of iron five feet long and two inches in diameter. A piece of steel was welded on the top end three inches in diameter for the purpose of tamping the dirt. The bottom end was tapered into a sharp blade eighteen inches long and four inches wide to chip at the hard soil.

The post was carefully dropped in and buried. A shovel full of dirt was dropped into the hole on each side of the post and then the crowbar was used to tamp the dirt securely. This was done alternately until the hole was full. Over time the wind blew the soil away leaving a low spot by the post starting a rotting procedure from moisture that collected around the post. They needed to be replaced every five years because a lot of posts were railroad ties. We split the railroad tie down the middle making it smaller so the hole didn't have to be so large.

[5] The power takeoff shaft makes the machinery move. As the tractor turned the auger it pulled the dirt up out of the ground. The operator on the tractor had to lift the auger up often or the sandy soil sucked the auger down like quicksand and then the tractor would die. It was quite a job to dig out a buried auger. The power-take off shaft that runs the equipment didn't go in reverse. We had to use a shovel. If the soil was hard like clay and adobe it took a long time to dig a hole. The bottom part of the auger that dug the hole was sharp and needed to be sharpened when it became dull. In some places the soil would be adobe or clay on the top for eight to ten inches and then sand below.

[6] There were heavy runners three inches wide encircling the ends of the Fresno Scraper to let it glide easily over the ground. The runners in front were in a vertical position so when the dirt was emptied the Fresno Scraper would slide on the runners leaving the dirt where it

was needed. The runners were horizontal on the bottom side for the scraper to slide smoothly along the ground when it was full of dirt. A handle enabled people to have control so when the horses pulled the scraper it would dig into the ground and fill with dirt, then they pulled down on the handle to keep it from getting any fuller. When reaching their destination they lifted up on the handle. A rope was tied to the handle so it didn't hit the horses. If the handle hit the horses they started to run thinking that was what they were supposed to do.

[7] They drove the team beside the road where they were to put the fence. Every place that a post was to be set they stopped the team took out a post and while one person held it the other drove it into the ground with a sledgehammer. A sledgehammer has a ten pound steel-head on a two foot long handle. Had it not been for the wagon box, standing on the ground pounding those posts would have been hard to do as steel posts are six feet long.

Today farmers have a steel post driver. It is a piece of pipe large enough to easily slip over the post with a weight of ten pounds welded on the end. The heavier the weight the faster a post can be driven into the ground but the more energy it takes to lift it. There is a solid piece of steel welded to each side that are handles. Lifting up on the driver and then using force pulling down on it drives the post in the ground. It takes three or four good hits and the post is in the ground. When using the sledgehammer the top of the steel post eventually starts to split. With the steel post driver this doesn't happen.

[8] The front and back had three 1x12s and with two 1x6's spaced six to eight inches apart above them. The frames were fastened with 2x4s for stability and supported with 1x6s fastened to the sides and the bottom on an angle holding them upright. The frame for the floor was made with 2x6s and the floor was 1x12s. The runners under the rack and above the wheels were 4x12s. The sides were open for loading the feed. The wheels on the hayrack were wooden four feet in diameter and three inches wide. There was a metal piece in the center that went over the axle acting as a bearing. There was a heavy piece of steel that went around the circumference that rolled on the ground. These narrow wheels made it easier for the horses to pull the wagon in mud and deep snow.

[9] There was an inner tube repair kit with a special type of glue, a little cap with grader type corrugation, small patches and a larger one. Sometimes the hole was so small that we had to fill the inner tube with air and put it in water. The air escaping made bubbles letting us find the hole. After the tube dried we roughened the surface with the grader type device put the glue on ignited the glue just enough to heat the tube and put the patch on. The tire was put back together carefully to avoid pinching the inner tube or it would leak again. If the outside of the tire had a flaw we inserted a boot. This was a large firm rubber patch put on the inside of the tire between it and the inner tube to keep it from repeatedly going flat.

[10] A branding chute was made to hold the cattle. It can be made larger for the older livestock and smaller for the younger calves. There are bars on the sides that can be dropped down to where the brand needs to be. There is space for castrating and the nose of the cow can be held tight while it is being dehorned, vaccinated or ear tagged.

[11] A lever allowed us to adjust the speed for larger or smaller grains to drop through the tubes that put the grain in a row instead of letting it fall helter skelter. There were holes just above the tubes allowing us to see if the seed was falling in each row while the packing wheels covered the grain. The six horses were not strong enough for drills to be large. The small shears plowing the furrows, the weight of the grain and the heavy packing wheels

made a load. As tractors were invented and became bigger all the machinery was made larger allowing us to cover more ground in less time. Today one farmer can farm more land than one hundred did in the early 1900's.

[12] On all horse drawn farm machinery there was a drive wheel that ran on the ground making all the functional parts move except the corn cutter, rake and manure spreader that had a gear. The more moving parts on a piece of machinery the larger and heavier the drive wheel. It had pieces of angle iron bolted on an angle for traction that acted similar to chains on a vehicle when on the icy road.

The drive wheel needed to grip the ground because a gear with a driving chain turned another gear that made the piece of machinery work. Today a power-take-off-shaft does what the drive wheel did. The drive wheel turned a gear on the bar holding the planter boxes on the lister. These gears turned the flat disk in the box and planted the seeds. There was a shear making a row and then two disks that pushed the dirt away just before the corn or beans were dropped through a flex tube from the boxes. There was a hole between the flex tube and the planter box for us to see if seed was falling. It had two little wheels behind each row that were slanted that packed a small amount of soil over the seed. Planting the corn in this way didn't leave much soil around the plants.

[13] The knives were bolted to a wheel on an angle. This let the knives cut the corn just like the knives on the corn cutter. The cut corn fell onto flat heavy pieces of steel bolted to a wheel on the inside end of the cutter. The wheel rotated at such a high rate of speed it blew the corn all the way to the top. At the top of these pipes that were sixty feet high was a crescent moon shape pipe that put the ensilage back into the silo. The reason this pipe was open on the bottom was because sometimes the pipes in the silo got blocked and the ensilage just fell. Pipes the same size in diameter as the outside pipes were two-and-one-half-feet long and were fastened to the crescent moon pipe at the top for Dad to put the ensilage where he needed it. The pipes in the silo were fastened together with hooks to form a flex type tube light enough in weight that made it easy to unfasten on the go as the silo filled up. There was a rope on the bottom pipe that Dad fastened to the next pipe when he removed the bottom one. There was too much noise with the tractor running and the cutter cutting the corn blowing it up in the silo for Dad to get the attention of the people on the ground to stop cutting if he had trouble. The people on the ground always kept an eye on the top to make sure the pipes going down in the silo were always free. If this half-moon shaped pipe wasn't open and problems occurred in the silo all the pipes would get packed clear back down to the cutter. Should this happen all the pipes would have to be disassembled, cleaned out, and reassembled. That would have been a two or three day job because the force would have packed the ensilage.

[14] The corn cutter was pulled by one horse and had small wheels in the front and two larger wheels in the back. The back wheels on the one-row corn-cutter were far enough apart to span only one row while the back wheels on the two-row cutter were far enough apart to straddle two rows. A very sharp knife ran from the front to the back on an angle and as the horse pulled the cutter down the field it cut the complete stalk from just above the ground. The men sat on a box type seat catching the corn and when they had their arms full they tossed the corn behind them on a pile keeping the piles even with the other rows next to them with the tops in the same direction. This way when it was time to pick up the corn for the ensilage cutter we put two piles on the hayrack from both sides at the same time. Since tossing the corn behind them was done on the go the men had to be fast to empty their arms turning around in time to catch the next stalk.

183

[15] A "mower" had a drive wheel with a six-foot long sickle. The sickle had sharp pointed "V" shaped pieces of metal attached to a bar. Sometimes one of these blades on the sickle broke and had to be replaced. The sickle slid back and forth over another bar that was stationary and made from a much heavier piece of metal with guards that had slats for the blades to slide through and sometimes even one of those broke. These guards had a slot for the blades of the sickle to run back and forth protecting the sickle. The blades coincided with the guards. The guards were also pointed to guide the product to be cut into the sickle and to protect the cutting blades. A rod was welded to the edge of a wheel and the end of the sickle. As the wheel went round the offset steel pushed and pulled the sickle back and forth. Sickles were on all pieces of machinery, except the corn sled, that cut the feed but were much longer up to twelve feet. If something got caught and wouldn't let the sickle move the wheel stopped turning and then the horses couldn't pull the piece of machinery. This was also true with a tractor.

[16] When we were raking we put our foot on a petal to hold the teeth down so if we crossed a bump it wouldn't dump our load. On one wheel there were slots like a gear so when we wanted to dump the load we stepped on a different pedal. The pedal allowed a piece of iron to drop into the gear and lift up the teeth leaving the cargo. We then grabbed a handle to hold the teeth up until the load was dumped. There was a hook that we placed over this handle to hold the rake up when we traveled and not raking.

[17] It also had needles to take the twine or wire around the bale to be tied. The needles started out straight and then curved slightly until just before they were fastened to the baler. There was a large metal plunger that packed the feed into a square metal box. When the bale was completed it was pushed off the carrier by the next bale to land on the side so the twine or wire was not on the ground.

[18] There were spreaders with which to spread the poison. The spreader was on two wheels with a fifty-five-gallon barrel on the top. A gear was fixed so when the wheels rolled on the ground it turned another wheel right under the barrel that had a hole in the bottom for the poison to drop with a shutoff valve. The poison fell on a platform under the barrel. A wheel that had flat irons welded vertically to angle irons under this opening, whirled around throwing the poison where we wanted it. This was done until frost killed the grasshoppers and their eggs.

[19] Special feeders were one and one-half inches high and made to keep the hens from spilling the expensive grain. There were fourteen holes in the lids, seven on each side and were oblong in shape just large enough for the chicks to get their heads in to eat until they were four weeks old. These were made of metal and had grooves on the sides enabling us to slide the lids off and fill them with feed. As the chicks grew the feeders were changed. My brothers made feeders from 1x6s four feet long. The ends were higher cut in an A-frame with a piece of heavy wire or 2x2s that fastened from one end to the other on the top so the fowl couldn't get into the feed and scratch it out.

[20] To keep the baby chicks from drowning we had a special watering trough. The metal ones were fixed so we screwed a canning jar on them. We put medicated water in the jar, screwed the trough on and quickly inverted the jar. As the chickens drank and lowered the water level air would enter the jar and water ran out keeping the trough full. The part that

held the water was eight inches in diameter and a half-inch deep. When the metal one rusted we purchased glass bottoms.

As the chicks got bigger we also got larger watering troughs. They held five gallons of water with a trough four inches high on the bottom leaving a three-inch wide rim holding the water around the edge for chickens to drink from. After filling them with water there was a sleeve that slipped over the edge. As the chickens drank the water level lowered and air entered the container letting water keep the trough full. These were large enough for the old chickens.

[21] To singe the hair we took newspaper, lit it and dropped it in a bucket. Holding the chicken above the flame we turned it around letting the heat burn the hair but far enough away from the flame so it didn't brown the skin. Later we put a tablespoon of rubbing alcohol in a plate to singe the chicken. The flame was beautiful and had a nice smell, not like the newspaper.

[22] A-frame hog sheds were made for brood sows for them to have their litters. It was only four feet high and six feet square. Six inches from the bottom, a 2x4 was secured to the front and back These boards along with the sides of the A-frame allowed the baby pigs to get away from their mother when she went to lie down. Without this protection she lay on her babies killing them.

[23] Ours was a homemade device with a one-gallon can and an upside down T that was cut in the side at the bottom. A one-inch thick board was trimmed making it round to fit inside the can, and an oblong frame made out of 1x4s large enough for the can and a car jack to fit in. After the hot lard was put inside the can we put the board on and started to push down on the hot cracklings pressing out the lard. Placing the can in the frame and the jack upside down into the can we started to press the lard slowly so it drained out of the bottom. We couldn't press too fast or the lard came up over the board instead of running out the bottom. A sieve was on the top of the container catching the lard to strain the cracklings that fell through the hole. Lots of times the jack would "kick out", knocking everything out of the frame and making a mess. Working with the hot lard was a hazard.

[24] When the wind blew it turned the wheel that was mounted on the top of the tower. On the opposite side of the wheel was a tail making the wheel face toward the wind enabling it to pump water. There was a strong wire fastened to the wheel at the top of the windmill. It was fastened to a 2 x 2 five feet long at ground level in the corner of the tower allowing us to turn the wheel sideways thus stopping it from turning. When the tank was full and we didn't need water in the garden we shut the windmill off by pulling down on the 2 x 2. When the wind blew too hard we shut the windmill off to keep from tearing up the moving parts. There were gears fixed to the wheel and as it turned a piece was offset that moved it up and down. Fastened to this piece was a 2x2 that came to within six feet of the ground just above the pump with the handle. The pipes going down into the well were two inches in diameter. Inside the pipe was a rod usually one quarter inch in diameter and it depended on the depth to the water level as to how large the rod needed to be to carry all the water from the bottom to the top. This rod was fastened to a cylinder that was just below the water level and was two feet long and coincided in diameter with the pipe. The rod was fastened to the working parts of the cylinder and every time the rod came up it filled the cylinder with water that had check valves made of leathers that closed and stopped the water from going back down. As the rod came back up again it put more water into the pipe pushing the water that was in

the pipe higher and as the process was repeated water arrived at the surface. When we had to use the handle because the wind wasn't blowing we disconnected the rod that went into the well from the 2x2 and fastened the handle to the rod. The handle was three feet long and as we went up and down water came to the surface just like when the wind blew. The wells were covered with planks to support the people and livestock that walked on top. It was covered with a heavy piece of tin to keep dirt from falling into the well.

[25] The wheels were two and a half feet in diameter. He found a rod that was two inches in diameter. The wheels and the rod coincided with each other and were bent just right for Dad to put the wheels on this rod. The rod was four inches from the ground and was almost square and wide enough for Dad to fix a platform to hold a ten-gallon can. He bolted boards to the platform made from angle iron. The platform was balanced so when we lifted on the handle we weren't lifting a lot of weight. The handle was three and one-half-feet long and the handlebars were wide enough apart so we pulled it behind us. We pulled it to the cooler and filled the can with water and pulled it back. We used this cart to haul water to the pig-pen or barn but someone usually helped push it up the hill. One of the drawbacks was that the soil was so sandy and the wheels of the cart sank into the sand.

[26] The separator consisted of a large seven-gallon tank that held the milk, a bowl that sepa-rated the milk from the cream and two spouts for the milk and cream to exit out of the sepa-rator into their respective containers. It had a large crank that was turned at one round per second and it took time to pick up speed because the bowl was of heavy metal. On the other side of the separator was a two-foot in diameter wheel with cogs. (This wheel was open on the oldest separators but later ones were enclosed because they were dangerous.) These cogs turned a wheel inside the separator with gears that fastened to a rod that came up out of the separator. It was one inch in diameter with a slot in the top to hold the bowl while it rotated. The bowl had to be rotating at a correct speed before the flow of milk was started. When it rotated at a high rate of speed the cream being lighter than milk came out of the upper spout and the milk from the lower one. With the disks and centrifugal force the cream was separated from the milk. Containers were placed under each separate spout to catch the milk and cream. An arm with a round piece of metal was attached to the separator on which to put the cream container. A bucket was on the floor to catch the milk.

The bowl consisted of several parts. The bottom part was ten inches high and the bottom half was in a cone shape for the disks. The very bottom was two inches wide and the out-side was three inches high. There was a round rubber seal to secure the top and the bottom so milk wouldn't run all over. Just below the disks was a piece of metal fixed for us to fas-ten a rod with which to pull all the disks out at one time. There were thirty-two cone shaped disks in the bowl four inches high and had a large hole in the center with three notches. The bottom piece of the bowl was built to coincide with the notches holding the disks in place to keep them rotating with the spinning bowl. The disks had small flat spacers welded between them for the milk to flow through and had three holes one-half inch in diameter to remove them from the bowl. Another cone shaped piece went on the disks and then went straight up to the top so everything could be secured tightly. The top part that covered all the disks was shaped to coincide with the bottom and had two holes in the upper side, one slightly larger for the milk and the other right above for the cream. In the side of the smaller hole was an adjustable screw. This allowed us to adjust the butter fat content for richer cream, or a lower test and thinner cream. A little groove was notched in the top of the bottom part of the bowl and an arrow was on a round nut letting us know exactly how much to tighten keeping the two pieces secure for satisfactory results. A special wrench with two spikes went into holes that were made in the round nut for us to secure the two pieces together. A place was fixed under the tank to hold the bowl while we tightened or loosened the nut.

[27] "Kickers" are two "U" shaped pieces of metal connected by a chain. The "U" part was placed over the back legs just above the second joint, or knee. The chain was adjustable so the legs were held together. The chain on the "U" shaped piece that was on the leg away from us was welded securely. The other "U" shaped piece had a hole with a slot in it so we pulled the chain through the hole while tightening it. We then hooked it in the slot to secure the legs. We had two pair of kickers so when more were needed we used rope. We put this in the same place on the cows' legs. The rope was wrapped around the far leg then crossed between the legs and wrapped around the leg near us and tied. The legs had to be pulled snugly or they sometimes kicked with both feet or even fell over. If this happened we had to start all over again.

[28] There was a gear on the rear wheel and when we arrived in the field we moved a lever that connected the gears making the spreader work. In the back, on the floor was a solid rod the width of the box with a gear on each end that went into chains that ran on each side of the box. Bolted to these chains were 2x4s and as the gear turned, it pulled the manure to the back. A wheel with eight-inch long pieces of very heavy wire secured to eight 2x2s turning in the opposite direction of a paddle wheel threw the manure in the air twenty feet wide. We did this in our spare time in the spring before we went to work in the field.